WINNING AT RETIREMENT

The **RETIREES GUIDE** to
SAVING YOUR RETIREMENT from:
Losses, Fees, Spousal Poverty,
and Going Broke in a Nursing Home!

Philip Richardson | George Sheets

Winning at Retirement

The Retirees Guide to Saving Your Retirement from:
Losses, Fees, Spousal Poverty, and Going Broke in a Nursing Home!

© 2018 Philip Richardson and George Sheets. All rights reserved.

Senior Tax Strategies
450 Murry HIll Drive
Lancaster, PA 17601

1642 South Market Street
Elizabethtown, PA 17022

(717) 394-0840
www.SeniorTaxStrategies.com

Printed in the United States of America.

ISBN-13: 978-1-946203-21-2

—Disclaimer—

www.PaperbackExpert.com

Table of Contents

Introduction

This book is designed to help you navigate the financial difficulties ahead of your golden years. You'll find countless tips in the following pages that are designed to protect your assets, so they're available for you and your loved ones.

But before I get to that, I want to start this book on a personal note and introduce you to a woman I got to know very well, named Helen Yuerhs.

Helen served as a nurse in World War II. She was an officer—a captain—though she never saw active duty. Helen did her service in Alaska, where she met a young sergeant named Ormond, who happened to be from the same area of Milwaukee as her. They snuck around together to avoid getting in trouble for fraternization between officers. After the war, they married.

That period of her life was so significant that, after she developed dementia in the later years of her life, she began to believe that she was just going away to her service again. She would often say, "If I knew I wasn't going to see my parents again, I never would've left home." In her mind, at that point, she was an eighteen-year-old nursing student, away from home for the first time. I can remember her coming up to me as if I were the hospital administrator, making reports, and telling me about her rounds, and just believing that she was in fact in a hospital, taking care of patients.

After the war, Helen and Ormond moved to Syracuse, where they settled down and raised their kids. Ormond got work doing the accounts for a life insurance firm. Helen, as you can imagine, remained a nurse until she retired.

They lived in the same house in Syracuse for the rest of Ormond's life. In that house, they raised their five children, including their youngest, Cathy, who would become my wife.

Helen was an incredible woman with a great story to tell, but for the purposes of this book, her story really begins later, when she and Ormond had done their job as parents and workers and were well into their retirement years. At that time, Cathy and I lived in Elizabethtown, Pennsylvania, and she was driving up to that old family house in Syracuse every weekend to take care of her aging parents.

Now, that's a five-hour drive, each way. The commute was quite a lot to ask from a young woman expecting her first child, but my wife was determined to make it. I've always admired how deeply she cares about people; she got that from her mother, I'd imagine.

At some point, after months of these commutes, I said to Cathy, "You know what? We have a big home here; maybe your parents should come and live with us. That would keep you from having to run up there, exhausting yourself every weekend."

Cathy loved the idea, so we decided to test the waters. At that point, we didn't have any firm plans, just a desire to see how Helen and Ormond felt about the idea.

So, we went up one Memorial Day weekend to lay out a tentative plan to see how they would take it. When we arrived, I sat down with Ormond and suggested that maybe it was time to think about them moving down with us. He was polite as always and heard me out, but he was noncommittal. We had a pleasant dinner and a nice evening all together, and the next day, he quietly passed away in the house. I guess his mind was made up; he wasn't going.

That was tragic enough for all of us, but unfortunately, we weren't able to focus on that tragedy because we had to decide what to do about Helen with no time to prepare. You can probably guess by now what choice we made: we went ahead with our plan to move her in with us.

We had hoped, when we set upon that course, to enjoy a few years in Helen's company. She could be fun and charming, and besides, we had a child on the way. We'd initially thought that Helen could lend a hand now our family was expanding.

It'll be nice to have some help around the house, we told each other. Maybe Helen can watch the children, we thought. Unfortunately, none of that ever panned out.

Right from the get-go, things were not right with Helen. I don't know if it was the shock of losing Ormond, or the shock of moving, or simply that she'd been able to hide the signs better when she was in her own home, but very quickly it became clear that Helen's mental health was not as good as we'd thought. She had memory deficits, which were severe enough that we couldn't allow her to make grilled cheese because she'd forget to turn the stove off. Very simple tasks became problematic for her. We ended up having to watch Helen full-time, and develop strategies for her. All while we were becoming parents for the first time.

Somehow, we managed. Helen lived with us for eight and a half years, and we somehow managed to take care of her and to have our three wonderful children. But, it wasn't easy. In fact, things got progressively more difficult as time went on. If this were a book about how to deal with a person with senile dementia, I could fill up entire volumes full of funny and not so funny stories about dealing with a person who has a memory deficit.

For instance, we used to go to Panera after church on Sunday, and Panera's very crowded. You have to sit close together, and Helen, one time, actually reached over to somebody else's platter and helped herself to their lunch while they were sitting there. We paid for two families' lunches that day.

Another time, we were at a sushi restaurant in the mall with Helen. The waiter brought over a dish and set it on the table, and Helen, who was always hungry, immediately grabbed something off of it. The waiter stopped back, and he said, "Oh, this wasn't for your table. It was for somebody else," but she had already eaten it. As soon as the guy left, she turned to us and, seemingly forgetting we were in a sushi restaurant, said, "You wouldn't have liked it because it tasted fishy."

Those are moments that make you laugh later, but they can be hard at the time. It is difficult to watch someone degenerate in front of you, to lose some of their dignity. This was especially true for someone like Helen, who had so much of it before. It makes you realize that something is wrong that isn't going to be fixed, and that requires you to make some lifestyle changes. So, we stopped going to restaurants. We stopped going anywhere where she might make those sorts of mistakes. She was, at that point, like a small child; we had to watch her and watch out for her constantly.

Life in our home was much the same. We had to actually turn the lock around in our front door so that we (or rather she) were locked in. To get out of our house, you had to use the key. To come in our house, you could just open the door and walk in. That was to prevent Helen from running away down the street, which she had done before. On one occasion, the police had to bring her back. Again, it was like having a fourth child in the house.

That's what the care of an elderly family member looks like. That's what the future can look like for you and for your loved ones if you don't take the proper steps now to prepare for it.

Those who are charged with the care have to change their whole lives. Even when it's willingly taken on, it's a heavy burden, and that burden is all the heavier when there isn't money available to get the help someone needs. At that time, Cathy and I didn't have the funds to get regular at-home care for Helen. We certainly didn't have the funds to put her in a facility where she would have been better taken care of. Hellen also didn't have the funds left over to do it. She'd worked hard and saved well throughout her life, but after five kids, the money was all spent. It would've been a real help if somebody had had the funds to help ease the work of taking care of her, but we didn't know how to get the money together.

As it turns out, the money was available that whole time. We just didn't know it. After Helen went to the nursing home, we found out that because of her service in World War II, she was able to qualify for what is called the Aid and Attendance Benefit. Because of her service, her children, namely my wife, would have been entitled to $2,600 a month, which we could've used to pay for people to take her mom out on day trips, to send her away to daycare centers, and basically to provide relief for us during the day. Over eight-and-a-half years, we missed out on about a $176,000 of benefit that the government would've paid to help her daughter take care of her.

Once we realized that was possible, and that we had missed out, Cathy and I sat down and asked each other some tough questions, chiefly among them: how could we be serving the senior market and not realize that this benefit was available? So, Cathy and I both went and got training on the Aid and Attendance Benefit and Medicaid planning.

We discovered pretty quickly just why we'd never heard of these benefits: no one is interested in learning about them and spreading the word. In our county, there were perhaps only three people that really understood the ins and out of this Medicaid and Aid and Attendance Benefit planning, and Cathy and I were two of them. Because of the lessons we learned from our experience with Helen, we've helped a lot of more people through our senior practice. We've shown numerous clients how to use them in their own family to provide care where they weren't otherwise able to do it.

Helen lived another eight years in the nursing home and passed away when she was 94. She lived an incredible life that was full of joyous moments, but the last 16 years were hard on her and her family.

I am starting this book with Helen's story because I want you to know that these issues are personal for me. My wife and I are in this business not to make a fortune but to help families avoid the struggles we went through with her mother. Helen was a wonderful woman, a veteran, a life-long nurse, and a great mother. She deserved the very best at the end. We want to make sure you and your family get the very best.

That's Cathy's and my life-long mission, although it took us a while to come to it. We're both 55, and we didn't start out working in senior planning. Our story is a little less of a straight road.

Now that you've gotten to know Helen, let me tell you a little about Cathy and me. I'm a graduate of Penn State University—the same school my eldest, Jordyn, is going to now. Out of college, I was a director of hotel, restaurant, and institutional management for Marriott. It was my job to run their hospital and nursing home food service in Connecticut, and later in New York and Pennsylvania. After all, someone has to prepare the food for nursing homes, and often it's a place like Marriott. So, you see, I was already somewhat involved in the world of elderly care, even if it wasn't yet from a financial perspective.

Cathy, it turns out, was also involved with that world from an early stage. In fact, that's how we met. When I was in Sharon, Connecticut, working with Sharon Hospital, she was the dietician who came to work for me as part of the Marriott deal.

In case you didn't know, Sharon is a very small town, and just like the military, corporations don't like it when you fraternize with other employees. So, like Helen and Ormond before us, we had to sneak around for a bit while we got to know each other. We kept our relationship a secret until we got married after our move to New York.

That move wouldn't be our last either. About every two years, I would get transferred to a new account working for Marriott. Marriott loved to move me around because I'm a fixer—it's my specialty. So, every two years or so, we would have to settle into a new town where I'd be given some problems to fix. Once I'd done that, off we'd go again to the next set of problems somewhere else.

I was good at what I was doing, but I wanted to get back to central Pennsylvania. So, when an opportunity came up to transfer and run Holy Spirit Hospital in Camp Hill, which is about 40 minutes from where we live now, we took it. I did that for about a year and a half, but I was burned out by that industry. I wanted to do something else with my life, something that would allow Cathy and I to settle and to help people directly. It was at that point, I decided to transition into financial services.

During that time, Cathy was also doing some transitioning. She started her own business being a consultant dietician, which meant she would go independently into nursing homes and do nutritional intervention for residents. She had four or five accounts in the area, and she was doing quite well. Then, she got pregnant, and things were looking very promising for us.

It was at that point that Ormond passed and Helen came to live with us. Suddenly, things weren't quite as rosy-looking. We had Cathy's mom and our first child, and I had gone into a new career in financial services, which wasn't quite panning out financially at the time.

I think I made $14,000 my first year in the business. It was not a roaring success by any means. Fortunately, Cathy was still earning an income, and our needs were pretty low, so we were able to survive.

I suppose a lot of people would have given up and gone back to the security a place like Marriott can give, but we were determined. Cathy and I knew how we wanted to help people, and we were going to do it, no matter the obstacles.

It took probably five years before my income was at a comfortable level, but every year I was getting better at what I was doing, even if I was getting fed up with the business angles I was encountering. When I started out, I was working for New England Financial, where I tried to offer life insurance to young people—a very difficult sale to make. More importantly, what I soon discovered is when you work for a company, whether it be one of the big name companies or something smaller and more local, you're not really working for the client. You're working for that company. When they tell you that you have to offer this or that, that's what you have to offer, whether it's in the client's best interest or not.

I couldn't get over that. The idea that my job was to offer what would be most beneficial to the business and not what was most beneficial to my clients. Why would they come to me if I wasn't looking out for them? I was getting into the business to help people. So, I quit. It was another struggle for the family, but I decided to branch out on my own.

I moved into the area I was really interested in—senior finances—and started on the long road to building up a client base. To help me make a name for myself without the help of a business, I decided to try to do some seminars to show people some useful tips while I also demonstrated that I knew what I was talking about and I could really help them. I ended up having some success at that.

But seminars are expensive, and you don't always get people to show. People are busy, after all, and it's hard to really pack in the seats when you want to talk about finances. As you'll see throughout this book, a lot of people try to avoid dealing with their finances as long as possible. Even though the advice I was offering was solid, people would pass right by because they just didn't want to spend their evening thinking about their difficult money situation.

Being a fixer, I knew I needed a new strategy. I decided that instead of paying all this money to convince people to come to my office so I could look at their tax return, I would just put a sign on my back and stand on a street corner, offering seniors a $50 deal if they let me look at their tax return.

That's when I started Senior Tax Strategies. I grew from no tax clients in 1999 to the business today, which does 2000 tax returns a year. And for years, that was our main driver of prospects: people would come in for taxes. We would do their tax returns, but then we would talk to them about their money and different ways they could pay less on taxes. That's where our real interest is, not just saving a little money for you this year but finding ways to make sure you have money in ten years, twenty years, all the way until the end, and then that there's something left over for your family.

Again, this is a personal mission for me. My parents never had much money. We did okay, but we were never well off by any means. When I was growing up, my parents would try to get financial advice, for college, for insurance, for anything. They never felt they got great advice. And in hindsight, listening to the stories they tell, I've never felt they got great advice either because of the kind of people they were working with. When I got into the business, I did so primarily as a way to help people get good financial advice that was in their best interest.

Most advisors hold themselves—and are held by others—to a much lower standard, both legally and ethically. They aren't looking out for you first. They can't. They have to look out for their company first and foremost. That was the first lesson I learned about the financial industry, and it's stuck with me.

I don't like that system. I never liked having a company be my top priority when I worked for one, that's why I risked everything to become independent. If I was going to be giving financial advice, that's not how I wanted to do it because that's not how I'd want to get it myself. I would want to get it from someone who was actually able to offer whatever they thought was going be in my best interest, regardless of how it helped or hurt a big corporation. I would hope that it would be the sort of strategies they would offer themselves if they were going to offer it to me.

Let me put that more plainly. If I offer you a financial product to solve your issue when I work with you, I already own that financial product or something very similar in my own portfolio. I'm not a financial hypocrite. I provide for myself exactly what I provide for my clients. If I didn't provide it for myself, I certainly wouldn't provide it to someone else. I was just not raised that way.

I'm very centered in that focus, that whatever I'm offering has to be the top value in the industry for the client. That's what I've always strived to do. Because of that, I have very loyal clients, many of whom have been with me going back even to when I originally started the business.

As an independent, I'm able to find what is in your best interest and offer it to you without having to worry about what financial products my boss wants me to be pushing.

That's not to say I don't have biases—of course I do. But my biases, I think, fit the demographic that I work with; I do not want you to have less money next year than you have this year. Whatever we offer you at my business, you have a guarantee of no losses. I want you to make as much money as you possibly, and safely, can. I want you to be in a position that if there are gains, you're capturing as much of those as you possibly can. Once we capture them, we do not want to give them back. So, my biases are as follows: safety first, guarantees on your money, and always having more money year after year going forward.

Those biases have a singular focus: I want to make sure you are not in Helen's position when the time comes. I want you to have all the money you need for your own care and all the money you can for your family after you pass. That's what separates me from other people in the industry.

In essence, what I want this book to do for you is to show you just how much bad financial advice you've gotten so far in your life, and also how many good options are out there for you. If you read it, this book will allow you to understand how I'm able to ensure your life savings and protect them. That's my main focus. I utilize strategies that allow me to say to you, with complete certainty, that regardless of what the stock market does, you're not going to have any years where you have less money than the year before. You have 100% safety.

I want to make sure that you have an income from your retirement savings that will last throughout your lifetime, so there are no scrimping and worrying years ahead. There's nothing worse than living longer than your income. That is not a great recipe for retirement success. For as long as you live after running out of money, you will regret the choices you make (or don't make) now if that ever comes to pass. There's no doubt about it.

Being financially prepared for the future isn't just about having enough money to live on, though. That's why I also want to make sure you are financially ready should you find yourself with deteriorating health. How can we best position you so that if that eventuality happens to you or your spouse, you have the best resources and plan available to pay for those unforeseen circumstances? How can we make sure what happened to Helen doesn't happen to you and your family? That's the next step.

Finally, I want to make sure that the money you don't consume during your lifetime, the money that you leave behind for your heirs, can pass in the most tax-efficient manner possible. Of the funds that are left, I want to make sure that your main beneficiary is not going to be the IRS. That means making sure that you are paying, even with your current income, the lowest tax rate possible on your money. How can you improve your income situation and, at the same time, decrease the amount of taxes that you're paying on that income? That's a problem I want to solve for you.

While you read this book, I want you to ask yourself a few important questions:

- Has any financial advisor ever shown you how to invest without the market risk and with the ability to provide protection from creditors?

- Has any financial advisor ever shown you how much income is at risk if your spouse predeceases you, and if they have, have they told you how they would replace that lost income to your family?

- Has any advisor ever shown you that the IRS has provided an exit strategy on your IRAs and annuities?

- Has any advisor ever reviewed with you the methodology for creating a tax-free estate from your IRAs?

- Do you completely and fully understand all of the risk associated with your investments when your advisor invests your money?

These are important questions, and I think you'll find the answers are not going to be to your liking. The truth is, your advisor may not even know that much more about investments than you do. They might have had 20 hours of training, where they learned how to talk around you in circles, but don't assume they actually understand the risks that you're taking when it comes to going, say, from stocks into bonds. If they can't articulate the potential pitfalls that either of those kinds of investments have, especially in today's environment with a sky-high stock market valuation and basement bottom interest rates, then it's time to consider finding someone who can.

If you read this book, you're going to find out that there are far better answers to those questions than your current advisor has been giving you. I can help protect you from the issues that real-world seniors have from the time they retire to the time of their death. Together, we can make sure we solve all the complex issues that people have to endure after they finish working. Together, we can make sure your golden years are golden, and there are no rough years ahead.

Chapter 1

Eliminate Taxes and Protect Your Income

I want to tell you upfront that I'm not a very good salesperson. I can never figure out how to sell something to somebody who doesn't want to buy it. Some people can do that. Some people can sell broken down cars or useless devices or bad financial advice. That's not me.

The only way I've figured out how to sell anything is to get you to the point where you can recognize your own problem, even if you've never recognized that problem before. Then, I can offer you the best solution for you. I don't know how to sell you something you don't want or something that isn't the best solution. All I can do is lay it out for you and let you decide.

So, with that in mind, I'd like to open this first chapter by asking you a few questions to get you thinking in the right frame of mind.

Just answer the questions as honestly as you can, and we'll go over them afterward.

- What two things in life are certain?

- If in the course of living you do not consume all of your money, how much of what's left behind do you want your beneficiaries to share with the IRS?

- If it were possible to morally, legally, and ethically disinherit the IRS, would you let me show you how to do that?

This first question is an easy one. We all know that the two things in life that are certain are death and taxes. And that's true. We know that those are certainties in life, even if nothing else is.

Now, I can't do anything about the death part. I can, however, certainly talk to you about taxes, but only if you're brave enough to embrace the part I can't help you out with: your own mortality. You have to recognize the fact that you're not getting out of this life alive, nor can you get out and take all your stuff. Once you truly recognize that fact, we can begin the process of becoming brave about the decisions you are going to make going forward. At that point, we can start to make wise decisions that will benefit you and your family while you're alive and after you're gone.

I want to highlight what I just said above. It's both brave and wise to face your mortality and plan ahead. Looking to take care of yourself all the way to the end and your family afterward, is the best way to be brave and wise at your time of life. I don't want for one second to suggest that is easy. It isn't. And the fact you're willing to do so is admirable.

Once we've accepted the need to be brave and wise and face the inevitable ahead, we can look at the second question, which also deals with taxes. Essentially, how much of what you have left at the end of your life would you like to split with the IRS?

I know the ideal answer is "none," but we all know the IRS is getting something. My goal is to make sure that something is as small as possible. To illustrate how we can make that happen, I want to introduce you to a little aid I like to use that can help us organize your finances. It's called the five buckets. Imagine these five buckets in front of you, and each of them is filled with parts of your income.

Now Bucket

This is where the money you are spending right now goes. This is your cost of living stuff. Your car payment, your mortgage, your food budget. All the money you need to get through this week, this month, this year. We aren't really going to talk much about this bucket in this book because I don't take anything from it. Part of my job is to make sure you have more than enough money to live on without using any of that money. A lot of financial advisors are trying to get money out of you that's in your Now Bucket. I'm not one of them. That's not what I do.

Later Bucket

This is where the money you've put aside that you plan to spend in the future goes. That includes vacations, a new car, those expensive Christmas gifts you want to buy the family this year. As far as I'm concerned, that money is already spent, and just like the Now Bucket money, I have nothing to do with it. You've already spent that. I can't spend it, you've already spent it.

Never Bucket

This is where the money you've put aside for a rainy day as well as the money you mean to pass on to your family goes. At your age, that rainy day is probably going to be long-term care for you or your spouse. It's with this bucket that things start to get interesting.

So, let me ask you: if either of you needed long-term care or any other kind of care, would you spend every penny you had to make sure you or your spouse was taken care of? Of course you would. And if there was money left over, you'd want it to go to your kids or other benefactors, right? Of course, but that's not how the IRS sees it.

This money is important, and we need to protect it. It's my job to help you manage this money in a way that allows you to make it grow without taking any risks.

Taxes Bucket

This is all the money the IRS plans to get from you. It's not really your bucket. You just take it with you and pour out whatever is in there right on the IRS's porch. Obviously, we want to keep this bucket as close to empty as possible.

Harvest Bucket

This is where your gains made at this stage of your life will go, at least if you follow the strategies in this book. We'll talk about this bucket in a moment.

Again, put those first two buckets out of your mind. I won't ever touch those. That's your money, and I won't be advising you how to spend it, either in this book or in person. But let's get back to that Never Bucket.

Imagine you're holding your Never Bucket in your hands right now. It's heavy right now because it's full of your rainy day funds, your IRAs, the money you've tucked away for your family after your passing. At this point, it's filled to the brim.

But not for long. Because here comes the taxman, and he says to you, "That's a very nice, full bucket you have there. Just let me know when you start emptying it because you'll need to pour quite a bit out for me as well at the same time. Once you get started, you just go ahead and tell me when to stop pouring it into the Tax Bucket. Just say when you've had enough taxes because if you don't say anything, I'll just go ahead and take it all."

How fast are you going to yell stop? Right away, I bet.

Since we know already that you are a person who understands that you have a mortality limit, that you want to make wise decisions relating to your and your family's future, and that you don't want to pay taxes, now we can start talking business. Now you're becoming somebody I can help.

We know you don't want all that Never Bucket money to go to the IRS. Of course you don't. No one does, but most people think they don't have a choice. Fortunately for you, that is exactly where most people are wrong, because there's an out.

Look at question three above. If it were possible to show you how to legally and morally disinherit the IRS, would that be something you'd want me to do for you? Look at that Never Bucket again, now look at the Tax Bucket. Would you be willing to follow a few simple, legal strategies to make sure that Never Bucket stays full and the Tax Bucket stays as close to empty as possible? Are you willing to give me a little time to show you how to do it?

I'm going to take a wild guess and assume that if you're still reading, the answer is "yes."

So, how do we do it? How do we save as much of this money as possible so that it's there for when you or your benefactors need it?

The answer is what I call the **5% Solution**.

With the **5% Solution**, I don't need every penny you have in your Never Bucket to provide you with the funds you'll need in the future. In fact, I need very little. Just about, you guessed it,

5%. Before getting into the details, though, so I can explain this better, why don't we enjoy a short story about a farmer and an IRS agent?

The IRS agent in this story is young, just starting out in the job, and he's anxious to make a good impression on everyone he meets. Among the first places he goes is a farmer's house. The farmer is out back, getting ready to plant the spring crops. He's got ten bushels of seeds to plant, so he's trying to put the IRS agent off. He's busy, and no one wants to take time out of their day to deal with the IRS. He's got to get the seeds in the ground.

This IRS agent, though he's polite and eager to be liked, is very persistent, and he says, "Listen, I have to collect some taxes. I know you don't want me to do it now, but let me make a quick deal with you. If you pay tax on these seeds right here, I won't come back in the fall and make you pay tax on the harvest. How does that sound for a deal, Mr. Farmer?"

The farmer, being a very smart individual, says, without hesitation, "I'll pay tax on the seeds." Which he does, and he considers that a very good bit of business done. The IRS agent has made his day.

That's because he's paying tax on ten bushels, versus the 1,000 bushels of harvest he would have been taxed on later.

I like that story because it illustrates what the **5% Solution** is all about. Just like in the story, what we want to do is to take some seed out of your Never Bucket now and pay tax on it so we can plant it and turn it into a huge tax-free harvest later. To do that, we just a little bit. In fact, all we need is that 5%.

What we do with that 5%, you'll discover in later chapters. For now, all you need to know is taking 5% from your Never Bucket can turn into a huge harvest in that fifth bucket, the Harvest Bucket. All we have to do is pay tax on that 5%, and then reinvest it in a smart, safe way to ensure your future harvest. Once we've done that, you'll need long-term care so, at your death, that Harvest Bucket is going to be full of a completely tax-free harvest.

Your family—not the IRS—is going to benefit from that. They'll be able to take care of their own income needs for the rest of their lives. All it takes is that 5%.

Now you can see why I call it the 5% Solution: I can solve all your financial concerns with just that 5% you were never planning to spend anyway.

I want to emphasize here that when we take out that 5%, we'll be setting it aside in such a way that you can't lose that money, no matter what happens. Not only won't you be able to lose a cent, you will almost certainly make money on it. But even if you don't, even if you never make a penny more, the very worst that can happen to you is that the money you have now will be nice and safe no matter when you or your loved ones need it.

That sounds pretty good, but I can imagine that you're feeling pretty skeptical right now. Trust me, I can understand that feeling. I've had a lot of clients come to me who initially felt they didn't need me. They already understood their finances just fine, and they weren't interested in any financial tips because they had it all figured out already. You'll meet a few of them later in this book.

Ultimately, I hear a lot of skepticism from people because of one major point: no one has ever told them possibilities like these exist. Well, my response to that point is always the same: there's a good reason why your previous advisors didn't tell you everything.

For one thing, the financial world is complex, and your advisors in the past may not have felt the need to explain everything to you that you need to know. I make a point of explaining everything, but many financial advisors feel differently. The reason they didn't explain everything is because 1) they may not have known, and 2) they probably couldn't sell these products to you even if they did know. That's right, they legally couldn't sell them to you. So, why would they tell you? That'd just be bad business.

The next question from my skeptical clients is obvious: why can't they sell these products to you? The reason has to do with licenses. Let's say you want to become a financial advisor, so you go to all the trouble of getting a license to offer mutual funds, which is where you think all the money is (for you, at least). Well, then you're stuck having to offer things that have fees associated with them. You're not going be able to offer things that don't have fees.

Once you can sell mutual funds, you're also locked into working for a brokerage firm, which will forbid you from selling things that don't have fees, even if you had the ability. If you want to also be a stockbroker, you need another license. Once you get that, you can sell mutual funds and you can buy and trade stocks for people, but you still can't sell the products I'm talking about.

To do that, you have to get more licensing, so you can become a registered investment adviser. However, a registered investment adviser generally is a fee-only person, so they don't take commissions, and these products are done on commission. If you've gone to all that effort to get licensed in all these different areas, and you make all your money from fees, are you going to offer your clients a safe, guaranteed annuity which only nets you a modest commission? No, you're going to offer everyone who walks in your door the products that have the biggest fees. If you do anything by a commission, you want it to be a big one. After all, you've gone through a lot of trouble and you want to make your money back now. It's understandable, but being understandable doesn't really help you. In a nutshell, that is why your broker and financial adviser are not going to offer a **5% Solution** product to you.

"Okay," my skeptical clients will say, "But then why hasn't the bank told me about all this?"

For the exact same reasons. The bank's business model is also built around fees. They're just like the rest. None of the financial advisors you've spoken to in your life have had any reason to tell you about these products. It all goes against their financial and business interests.

So then, what about the investment magazines? Why aren't they screaming about these options on every page? Well, the financial press gets paid by selling advertisements, and fee production companies mostly buy those advertisements. They pay for all the advertising in Money magazine and similar entities. Are those companies going to continue to buy ads if they get negative press that hurts their business? Unlikely. Fee-based companies want to make sure you stay in a fee-based environment so that they can earn the most amount of fees from you. They don't want articles that tell you something different is out there, so the magazines don't print them. It's as simple as that.

You have an entire financial complex where 90% of the people working are in the part of the industry where they can only offer fees. They can't do anything else. Even if they wanted to, they couldn't do anything else.

But they don't want to because it isn't in their interest. And it isn't in their interest because it isn't in their company's interest.

Basically, anyone working for a bank or a brokerage firm or an investment company works for that company first and for you second. Their allegiance is to their company—it has to be. The company pays their salary. The company pays their health insurance. The company pays for the food they put on the table and their kids' insurance as well. The company makes sure they have a nice house and a few weeks vacation every year. Even if they could legally sell you these products, they wouldn't do it.

Only independent advisors who have walked away from those big companies can offer these products. And independent advisors are rare because it is so hard to set up on your own. You have to work on your own, pay all your own bills, rent your own office space, and take on all the risks of running a business. I told you in the introduction how little money I was able to make going out on my own. That lasted five years. Being independent in the financial world is tough. But only someone who has taken on all that is able to offer you these products, because these products don't have any fees, they don't have any charges, and they have so many guarantees. It's a losing proposition for anyone else.

Now, not everybody who is independent offers you the very best of what's out there, so you do have to be careful. Just because they're independent doesn't mean they work like I do, and give you the very best of what's available. There are some pretty awful no fee services out there as well, that's for sure. There's always the best, and there's the worst, and you don't want to get the worst of anything.

That's why you've never heard of these options before. Even if you've worked with a great broker, they haven't been able to give you the kind of advice you need at your time of life.

Now that you understand why you haven't heard about this advice, it's time to start getting into how you can apply. To warm you up for what's ahead, test your knowledge about typical financial topics with the quiz below. These are things that we're going to be addressing in this book, but it's good for you to begin to think about them here and find out how well you understand how these issues work. The reality is that you may not understand your finances quite as well as you thought. And those misunderstandings can lead to real trouble later in life. That is unless you follow the advice in the next chapter.

Financial Quiz

1. If your beneficiaries inherit Traditional IRA Monies from you, the tax due by them will be?

    a. There will be no tax, IRA's pass to the beneficiaries in a step up basis.
    b. They will pay long-term capital gain tax.
    c. They will pay ordinary income tax but only on the earnings.
    d. All of the money is subject to ordinary income tax.

2. If your beneficiaries inherit non-qualified annuity monies from you, the tax due by them will be?

    a. The annuity funds pass tax free to my heirs, unless the estate is large enough to trigger federal estate taxes.
    b. They will pay long-term capital gain tax only on the gain.
    c. They will pay ordinary income tax only on the gain.

3. If your beneficiaries inherit corporate bonds, money markets or CD's from you which of the following is/are true:

    a. My heirs will not pay income tax or capital gain tax on these accounts.
    b. These funds get a step up basis and are tax-free.
    c. All of the interest is taxable when my heirs receive these accounts
    d. My heirs will pay long-term capital gain tax.

4. If Bob and Mary lose 30% in the stock market, how much must they gain to get back to zero?

    a. 30%
    b. 35%
    c. 43%
    d. 53%

5. If one spouse survives the other and both were drawing social security, (his $1,000 and hers $500) the following is generally true:

    a. The check for $500 a month will stop.
    b. The check for $1,000 a month will stop.
    c. The surviving spouse will receive $750.
    d. There will be no change.

senior consultants

6. Bob and Mary have been married for 48 years. Bob retires from Kraft Foods after 35 years of service. His pension is $2,000 per month. Bob chooses the most common pension option in the United States. Bob chose a pension that would leave his spouse:

    a. 100% of his pension
    b. 75% of his pension
    c. 50% of his pension
    d. 25% of his pension

7. Now, combine questions 5 and 6 and tell me how much annual income Mary will lose if she survives Bob?

    a. $12,000 a year
    b. $1,500 a month
    c. $6,000 a year
    d. $18,000 a year

8. Americans that are now 65 years of age or older, women tend to live longer than men. What percentage of the time does this happen?

    a. 70 - 85%
    b. 55 - 70%
    c. 40 - 55%
    d. 25 - 40%

9. The current per person Federal Estate Tax limit is approximately?

    a. $500,000
    b. $750,000
    c. $2,000,000
    d. $5,000,000

10. A revocable living trust protects my estate from liability lawsuits.

    a. True
    b. False

Chapter 2

Safe Money Savings

How did you do on the quiz? Whether you've proved to be an expert or found out you don't know all that much about your finances, there's plenty of reason for you to keep reading. As I said in the last chapter, there are plenty of so-called experts who don't know the strategies I'm about to highlight. It really is in your best interest to find out how to protect your assets today, tomorrow, and for the rest of your life.

To start off this chapter, I'd like to tell you another story; this one I call the tale of two brothers. These two brothers, Steve and Bill, are very similar. They work similar jobs, retire at similar ages, and have similar health concerns. They even retire with the same amount of savings, but crucially, they retire ten years apart. Steve retires in 1990, while Bill retires in 2000.

Take a look on the next page at how that little difference changes the entire financial outlook for each brother.

The lesson here is, if you get negativity in your investment portfolio early in retirement—as you can see Bill did—you run out of money and you have a very bad retirement. If you can earn money in your early years of retirement, then it doesn't matter what happens later, because you get over the hurdle, and you just make money hand over fist. You never have to worry about money again.

What did Bill do wrong that Steve did right? Nothing, except he trusted the stock market to provide for him, and he trusted it at a bad time. The bad news for you is, we're likely about to enter another bad time for the market.

Two Brothers
Two (Different) Retirements

- $500,000 in each IRA at retirement
- Both will use $30,000 annually for income
- Steve retires in <u>1990</u>
- Bill retires in <u>2000</u>
- The result?

INCOME AND SEQUENCE OF RETURNS

Steve
Retired in **1990**

Bill
Retired in **2000**

Year	Return	WD	Balance		Year	Return	WD	Balance
1990	-4.34%	$ 30,000	$ 449,602		2000	-6.18%	$ 30,000	$ 440,954
1991	20.32%	$ 30,000	$ 504,865		2001	-7.10%	$ 30,000	$ 381,776
1992	4.17%	$ 30,000	$ 494,667		2002	-16.76%	$ 30,000	$ 292,819
1993	13.72%	$ 30,000	$ 528,419		2003	25.32%	$ 30,000	$ 329,364
1994	2.14%	$ 30,000	$ 509,085		2004	3.15%	$ 30,000	$ 308,794
1995	33.45%	$ 30,000	$ 639,340		2005	-0.61%	$ 30,000	$ 277,094
1996	26.01%	$ 30,000	$ 767,829		2006	16.29%	$ 30,000	$ 287,345
1997	22.64%	$ 30,000	$ 904,873		2007	6.43%	$ 30,000	$ 273,892
1998	16.10%	$ 30,000	$ 1,015,728		2008	-33.84%	$ 30,000	$ 161,359
1999	25.22%	$ 30,000	$ 1,234,328		2009	18.82%	$ 30,000	$ 156,081

There's a way to avoid Bill's problems, though. My strategies let you avoid those losses, no matter when they occur. With the products I'm offering—which are called indexed annuities—you don't lose money because you can't lose money; you can only make money. Look again at Bill's finances. In the scenario I'm telling you about, if Bill had never lost that money, he'd be way ahead of the game, no matter when he retired.

That's true for you, too. No matter if you retire where there is no money to be made early, or there is money to be made hand over fist early. No matter what, you are still going benefit. You're not going to have to worry about your retirement account because it's going to take care of itself. You get all the benefits of the market with the security of knowing your money is not at risk.

We're now starting to see the benefit of thinking safely with money in retirement. My goal for your finances should be to protect yourself as much as possible while still participating in as many of the gains as you possibly can.

To show you the best way to do that, I want you to take a look at the American Equity Chart on the opposite page. That chart shows you, over the last 20 years, how well an equity indexed annuity has performed versus the S&P 500.

Take a look at the fluctuation in the S&P, the big rises and the big drops. The big rises mean a Steve retirement. The big drops are Bill retirements. Normally, you just don't know which one you're going to get, but I'll let you in on a little secret: we're due for a period of Bill retirements right about now.

The axiom of the stock market is "buy low, sell high." Well, once again, we're at an incredible high at this point. This is the time to be selling, not maintaining, and certainly not buying.

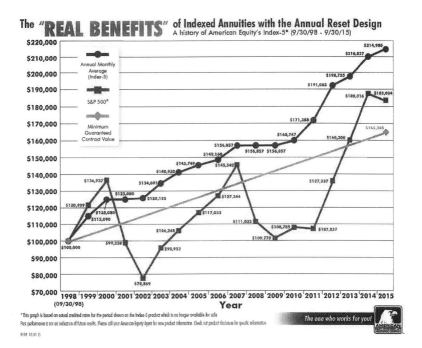

The "**REAL BENEFITS**" of Indexed Annuities with the Annual Reset Design
A history of American Equity's Index-5* (9/30/98 - 9/30/15)

You want to get out while the getting is good, and you want to lock in all of those gains forever.

The way you get out is by switching to an equity indexed annuity. See how well that performed in the chart? Sure, the highs are not as high, but there is no risk for you. In fact, an indexed annuity is the safest investment you can make, as you can see on the next page.

In the next few years, we're in for a double whammy, as rates go up and the stock market declines. Both bonds and returns on investments will be hammered, and if you're still using a traditional advisor, you won't have anyplace to go with your money. Forget about the taxman, the market will be coming for your savings then.

The fact is, you just can't know when that double whammy is going to hit. Markets go up and down. Recently, the market has been way up. When will it go down? You can't know if it will be tomorrow, in a year, or in three years, so why take a risk on it? Now is the time to reinvest your money safely so you are provided for long term. Now is the time to make sure you're a Steve and not a Bill.

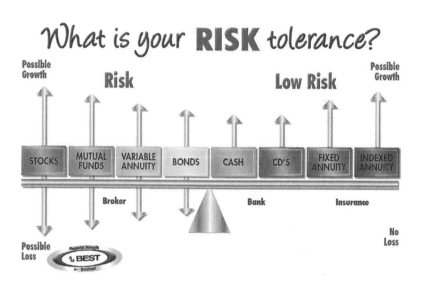

Of course, that's not what your financial advisor is going to tell you. That's because you can't make the changes you need to make if you stick with your broker and stick with the markets. Even if the market stays strong for longer than expected, you're still going to be losing money through your broker's fees. Those fees eat into your earning every single year. Think of it like this: when you use a broker, you're renting your gains because you're in a fee account. It's not real money, it's rented money.

With all that risk on your shoulders, you'd think you should be sharing the exposure, but that's not the case. You're taking all the risk, but you're giving your adviser a big chunk of any and every reward. It might be fairer if you only had to pay him if your investments went up, but you're paying him when they go up, when they go down, when they go sideways. It doesn't make any difference.

In 20 years, a financial advisor can make $100,000 on you, and if the stock market happened to drop 50% at that point, you would have made nothing in those 20 years. But he would still have made his $100,000 off of you. That doesn't seem fair at all to me. That's why I don't like to play by those rules.

I want to put your money in a place where it's safe, where the market going up helps you but the market going down doesn't hurt. I don't want you paying fees every year no matter how much money you've made or how much you've lost. That's why I don't charge fees. Nothing I offer has fees attached to it.

The gains you make with an indexed annuity are real money gains. You own those gains. You're not renting them temporarily, or leasing them. You own them.

You don't have to take my word that this is a smart strategy. There are plenty of well-known financial experts who have been advocating for these accounts for years, their views just don't get publicized. Take Suze Orman. Suze has plenty of good things to say about index annuities. According to her, "If you do not want to take any risks but still want to play the stock market, a good index annuity may be right for you."

That's you, right? You want to be safe and well-provided for like Steve, not Bill. Suze further repeats the point that an index annuity "cannot go down," and that while it does "limit your upside" it protects you "from a downturn."

Suze Orman isn't the only one to have caught on. Tony Robbins says the same thing. Tony considers a fixed index annuity to be the right choice for people entering the "second act of [their] lives" because it allows for a "great upside" while also providing "a guaranteed lifetime income."

I want to make clear to you that I'm not just selling you something I heard about from Tony Robbins. This is something I believe in so much that I have invested my own money in it, and the story of my investment speaks to how well an indexed annuity can do for you. In my case, I put money in an index annuity in March 2008. Well, in March 2009, the stock market was down 50%. Everyone else in the country was panicking, but not me. I hadn't lost a penny.

From March 2009 to March 2017, while the stock market has been rising steadily, my account is up 98%, and I can never lose that. If the market continues to grow through March 2018, I'll add that gain into my account, and I can never lose that either.

Think about that for a minute. In ten years, I'll certainly have made over 100% on my return of investment. And I can never lose any of that money. It's all mine. All that without a fee, all without an expense, all without a charge, and I'm free to walk away with all of my gains at the end of the year. Who else is offering you a product like that? No one.

So, indexed annuities are good enough for Sure Orman, and Tony Robbins, and me. But are they good enough for people outside the industry? Well, to answer that question, let me tell you about Bob and Mary.

Bob and Mary are clients of mine. When they came to me, they had a portfolio that consisted of about $200,000 in mutual funds and $200,000 in variable annuities. This wasn't money easily earned. To make that $400,000, they had both worked for nearly 50 years. Sometimes, when times were tough, Bob had worked two jobs. They did all they were supposed to, working hard and saving, and now that they were retiring, they wanted to reduce their risk, simplify their estate, and reduce their exposure to liability.

After attending one of my seminars, Bob and Mary came to me because they weren't satisfied with the answers they were getting from their broker. Under my advice, they moved their money out of variable annuities and mutual funds and into indexed annuities and life insurance (more on that later). Their principal is now fully protected from all downside risk in the market. Their potential earnings are still strong, and most important of all, they have more peace of mind regarding their life savings. It was a win on all sides, or at least, for everyone but their broker.

Here's the kicker, though, and the real reason I wanted to share this story: as we were in the process of moving these funds, their broker actually called and asked what they were doing. They explained that they wanted to move to accounts with less risk. He said "I can do that for you."

Bob responded, "then why haven't you already done it?"

That broker worked for one of the big brokerage firms, so when he said he could help Bob and Mary, Bob knew by then he was lying. Those guys are just not able to protect your money at this stage in life. With the tools in their tool box, they can either make you money or make your money safe. They can't do both like I can.

The safe money that still makes you money concept underlies everything that I do. It's a foundational issue. I want to make sure that you're secure, that you're safe, that you don't have to worry about your money.

Here's another story; this one is about Edward Jones. I had a client come in, and they actually worked for Edward Jones. They were an office clerical person. With Edward Jones, what the advisor does is very secretive. They don't share information with the office workers. The workers don't know how the advisor makes money or how much money they make. They don't share that.

But I know how it works, so when she came to ask for help, I told her, "Hey, you're paying a lot of fees." Her comment was, "No, I work for Edward Jones. They told me they were doing this without fees."

"Well," I said, "if that's true, I won't charge you to do the college planning for your family. That will save you $900."

A $900 bet with no downside was too good an offer to turn down, so she brought all of her statements in. Guess what? I won that bet. I categorically proved to her that they were charging her fees on her investment accounts.

Now, she had quite a bit of money. She had close to a million dollars with them that she had inherited and saved up. It was kind of ticking her off that they were charging her these fees when they told her they weren't. That's very typical of these companies. They were using a lot of high-cost mutual funds which have high commissionable fee structures. Do you have some of those in your account? If you're working with one of the big brokerage firms, you almost certainly do. Why do you have them? You didn't pick them; they picked them for you because they make the most money—for them!

This was really aggravating her, but she wasn't quite ready to make a change until she realized they were messing with her kids' college funds. She had money set aside for their education in a Pennsylvania 529 plan. A Pennsylvania 529 plan, however, doesn't pay broker commissions. So, her broker at Edward Jones had suggested to her that she take her money out of the Pennsylvania plan and put them in a Virginia plan. The only reason to do that is the Virginia plan will pay the broker commissions on the account.

Once she found that out, she not only gave me all of her money to manage, she went in and quit working for them as well.

Of course, most broker breakups are not as dramatic as that one, but advisors hate me just the same. After all, I know all their dirty secrets, and when it comes down to it, they cannot compete against what I'm selling. They do not have the ability. Working for the institutions they do, they can't offer you this stuff even if they wanted to, even if they were your brother-in-law. Even then, they couldn't come back and say, "I can do exactly what he's doing."

They cannot. For me, that's fantastic because I don't have any competition. Safe money savings is what I do, and no one beats me at it. Everything in my business revolves around it. It's a great way as a retiree to save your money and still make more.

Who can complain with making 100% on their money in 10 years? That didn't just happen to me. Every client I invested in 2008 has doubled their money. Every one of them. Hands down. Has your broker done that for you?

I bet not, and I bet they can't explain why, but I can. The answer comes down to one word: fiduciary.

A fiduciary is a legal standard that requires me to work in a client's best interest. I signed what's called a fiduciary pledge that says just that. What that means is that your interests have to come first for me, always, and I have to be able to prove that. For instance, unlike your broker, I have to disclose every conflict of interest that I have. Where your broker can hide fees like one did to my client at Edward Jones, I can't hide the fact that I get a commission. I have to disclose that. I also have to disclose the amount of commission I get. Go ahead and come into my office and ask me, I'll tell you straight. I'll lay out every where I can make a buck. I have to do that by law.

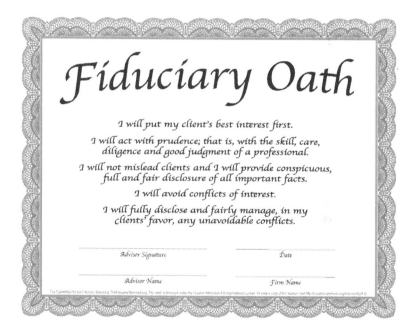

Fiduciary Oath

I will put my client's best interest first.

I will act with prudence; that is, with the skill, care, diligence and good judgment of a professional.

I will not mislead clients and I will provide conspicuous, full and fair disclosure of all important facts.

I will avoid conflicts of interest.

I will fully disclose and fairly manage, in my clients' favor, any unavoidable conflicts.

....
Advisor Signature   Date

....
Advisor Name   Firm Name

As a fiduciary, I also have to justify whatever I do for my clients. Whatever advice I give you, I have to prove that I thought it was in your best interest. I can be made to justify my decisions to a third party. If my clients are unhappy, they can demand that of me. That's not the case with your broker.

Being a fiduciary holds me to a legal standard that's way above that of your broker. Your broker just has to pass a suitability test. That means all they have to prove is that an investment was suitable for people in your situation to buy this. They don't have to prove that it was in your best interest to buy it.

Let me tell you, there is a big difference between what is suitable for you and what is best for you. That's why I spend so much time making sure I give you the best advice out there, that there is not a better product for your money than the one I'm offering right now.

If I get asked, "Why didn't you sell me this product or use that strategy? Is it because you made more money?"

The answer is always, "No. If that policy or strategy were better, I would be selling that."

My clients know all this, and yet, they still sometimes get suspicious. Which is good, it keeps me on my toes, and besides, I'm used to it. In fact, let me tell you the story of another client of mine, a client I'd had for ten year already at the time this happened.

At that point, my client decided to get remarried. Her new husband was kind of in the business, and he wanted to have a look over her finances as they started their life together.

So, I got a call one day, and it was my client on the other line, frantic.

"I can't believe you sold me this," she screamed into the phone, "You made 21% commission off of me. This is horrible. I have all these fees and expenses. I can't believe you did this to me."

I answered back calmly, "Wait a minute. Where's this coming from?"

Then she tells me, "Well, my husband..."

That was enough for me. I knew exactly where this was coming from. I've known quite a few amateur experts in my time who thought they knew better. So, I said to her, "Okay. No problem. Let me explain a few things. First of all, I wish I made 21% in commission. That would be fantastic for me if I did. I'd be a rich man then. Second, what do you care how much I make? You've doubled your money since you've been invested with me. So, what does it matter? Look at your account statement. It went from this, to this. You doubled your money."

"Oh," she said, already somewhat mollified. "Well, but what about the fees?"

"There are no fees. I don't charge fees, and I don't make 21%, but you did double your money."

She was still skeptical, so I said I'd come over and help explain it to her.

Which I did. I showed up at this house, and I was greeted by the new husband, who turns out to be a big guy. I started wondering at that point if I'd made a mistake, but when we got in the house, he came up to me and said, "You know, I have to apologize. I can't believe the unbelievable job you've done for my wife here. I was completely mistaken about you. I got bad information from another guy. This is wonderful. In fact, I want to mentor under you. I want to come and work for you, and I want you to teach me how you do this."

Of course, I wasn't a bit surprised by any of this (although I was a bit relieved), and I told him as much. I said, "That's how I work. I take care of my clients."

It was very nice to finally get him to validate the fact that we had done this great service for his new wife. That's the kind of work we do for everybody. Some recognize it, some don't. But no matter how they feel about it, we offer the same advantages and the same products to everyone.

After this chapter, I hope it's pretty clear it's the time to break up with your broker. I think I've laid out a pretty clear case here why that's necessary, but for some reason, I know many of you still don't want to go through with it.

I understand. It's like getting divorced. A lot of people want to avoid conflict, and your broker is very good at maximizing this and making you feel guilty for taking your money away. They'll tell you that you're crazy, you're going to lose money, you're being cheated. They tell you it's a scam.

Everything they can say, on an unrecorded line, they'll say. They'll never put it in writing, but if they can talk you out of it over the telephone, that's what they'll do. To help you along in this process, I've provide a little guide for you on the next page, just so you know what your broker is going to tell you, and why you shouldn't listen to them.

Your broker may have a lot of excuses and reasons, but it really all comes down to one thing: those fees. If you start with your broker with $100,000, and your broker charges a 2% fee, after 20 years, that broker is going to make over $100,000.

Essentially, your broker stands to lose $100,000 over the next 20 years. That's what your account means to him. Don't you think he's going to do everything in his power to prevent you from leaving? He doesn't want to give up that income stream. That's his livelihood. When you walk out the door, he is watching $100,000 leave. He's going to do everything he can to prevent that. That doesn't mean he's bad at his job, but it's something you have to be aware upfront.

If you're still afraid of upsetting your broker, I can understand that, and that's why I'll work directly to get your money transferred. Don't worry about it. I'll call the broker. I'm not afraid of him. I'll make him do what you want to do and get the money transferred to where you want to go with it.

What your Ex-

-Broker, -Banker, -Financial Planner, -Money Manager, -"Financial Guru" will say when you break up with them...

- **I have a product that will do something exactly like that.**
  If they do, and they usually don't, why did they wait until now to show it to you? Are they only acting in your best interest when they are losing your account?

- **There are a bunch of hidden fees in those products.**
  Our fees are optional, their fees are mandatory. All of our fees are disclosed in bold print, some of their fees are hidden or hard to find within the fine print of prospectuses which can be hundreds of pages long.

- **You don't get all of the market gains in that type of product.**
  True, but you don't participate in losses. If you have a 30% loss you need almost a 43% gain to get back to where you started.

- **The loss you have experienced is only a paper loss.**
  So when you have a gain do they say, "It's only a paper gain." Any loss you have requires you to recover from that loss before you can start earning again.

- **You don't want to tie up your money for long periods.**
  Other than the money you are spending today, the rest of your retirement money is always in a holding pattern. The question is, what is it doing to provide you guarantees or are you just hoping it will be there when you need it? As long as you have adequate emergency funds, you can let the rest of your money work for you.

- **It sounds too good to be true.**

  Just because your broker or banker didn't tell you about it doesn't make it untrue. Besides, annuities have been around for over 200 years and are state regulated by the Department of Insurance.

- **If this is so good, why aren't more people doing it?**

  The financial planning industry is dominated by fee based services and products. Moreover, this industry is heavily supported by the media through advertising dollars. Fortunately, the tide has started to turn. In an era of corruption, corporate greed, political malfeasance, international destabilization, and the threat of terror, retirees are looking for safety. Due to product enhancements and market risk, fixed annuity sales have been growing at an unprecedented rate.

- **I have been your money manager for decades.**

  Chances are your last job is not the same as the first job you had out of high school. You probably also don't live in your first home or drive the first car you bought. As your life changed so did your jobs, homes, and cars to meet your current needs. At this time in your life you need a financial professional that will secure your retirement with guarantees and lifetime income. If those needs have not been addressed in a meaningful way prior to us meeting, then it is time for a change.

The truth is that people who represent VARIABLE products rely on your annual fees and charges for their income. The second you move your money from their risk accounts to SAFE accounts, they stop collecting fees. Isn't it time to stop paying high fees? Isn't it time to protect your principal, lock in your gains, and develop a guaranteed strategy for lifetime income and/or legacy planning? It is time to end the game of chance. You need to stand firm and protect your hard earned retirement so you can sleep at night knowing you are no longer at risk to the uncertainty of the ups and downs of the market and economic volatility.

If you come into my office, I promise I'll pick my phone up and make that tough call for you. But you have to come into my office first.

Chapter 3

Disinherit the IRS

I've known a lot of people who can accept everything I've put in this book so far as true and who will still insist they don't need help. They've got it figured out, they tell me; they've got a plan.

One such couple came up to me once after a workshop. They were really excited about what they had learned, and they wanted to ask me some questions because they were going to be going away on a long vacation, and they had some concerns that just couldn't wait. They wanted to talk it over right then and there because they didn't have time to come in for an appointment.

Well, since I'm a pretty accessible guy, I agreed to hear out their questions and give them the best advice I could. They gave me an overview of their finances, and most of their questions were pretty easily answered. But then, they wanted to get into long-term planning, and I had to slow them down a bit.

"Before we get to far into that subject," I told them, "let me ask you a couple of questions, because my concern is that we haven't addressed the income needs for the surviving spouse."

I got a bit of a blank stare at this. As you know from chapter one, a lot of people don't like to recognize the only two certain things in life. They don't like to think about the fact their spouse may survive them, and what the world would look like without them. For them, bravery and wisdom are overrated, at least when it comes to that topic. So, I had to prod them a little.

I looked to the man and said, "Sir, what do you do for a living, or what did you do when you were working?"

He told me he had been a minister, but he was retired now.

"Great. And what kind of income do you have coming into your household?"

He mentioned that he had a pension, and that it was $4,000 a month.

"Well, that's great," I said, "and how do you take your pension?"

I knew right then there was going to be a problem. He sort of muttered around for a moment or pretended like he didn't understand. I honestly think he might have tried to play deaf if he thought he could get away with it, but his wife was right there and she seemed like a pretty straight shooter.

After giving her a glance, he finally said, "Well, I took my full pension."

Now, since I'm in the business I'm in, I know what that expression means. I understood it, and I could tell already that he understood it, but the disinterested look his wife was giving suggested that she didn't understand it.

But before I could address that, I had to get all the details, so I asked him what other income he had, and he said that he got about a thousand from Social Security, and his wife also got about a thousand a month.

"There you are," the wife told me, "We're getting $6,000 a month, just for the two of us. For the first time in our lives, we can afford to do everything we want. We're living the lifestyle we always wanted. We're very blessed."

If I were any less direct a person than I am, I might have just let the whole thing pass at that. It's horrible to crush someone's illusions. She looked very happy and proud of her husband, but I had to get her husband to tell her the truth and lay out what was ahead for her.

I'm a big fan of the truth, you see. I think that a spouse—any spouse—deserves to know what their future looks like with—and potentially without—their fellow spouse. So that meant I had to get her husband to explain to her what it meant when he said he "took his full pension."

I decided to deal with it head on and asked her, "Ma'am, excuse me, but do you know what it means that your husband took a full pension?"

She said, "No, I don't. We did it a long time ago, and I don't really know what that means."

She was completely innocent. It was heartbreaking, but I pressed on.

I said, "Sir, would you have any objections to telling your wife what you meant by that term, that you took your full pension?"

Now he was no longer shuffling around, he was looking at me in what I might call a way that was not very ministerial in nature, in a way that very clearly spelled out that he did, in fact, object.

So I added, "You know, it's important that she knows and that you discuss it with her. I can help both of you, but only if you are completely honest about this. Go ahead and tell her."

He turned to her, and he said, with surprising casualness, "Oh honey, it just means that at my death, you're not going to get my pension anymore."

Now, she didn't look so innocent and happy. She looked kind of devastated by this, and extremely surprised. Unfortunately, that was not surprising to me. This is, sadly, not that rare a situation for couples to be in. Sometimes, both parties don't know what their past financial decisions mean. They think they do, but then when the consequences come rolling along, they're blindsided.

Not that I blame them. Finances are difficult, and life is full of responsibilities. Think about it. Someone is retiring, there's all sorts of things to worry about, and then there are these papers to be signed, and often they are just shoved in front of one or both parties with someone saying, "Hey, just sign here. Don't worry about it. Don't read it, just sign it." Only later do they find out the situation they've put themselves in.

I don't know whether this minister's wife knew about it and she forgot, or if he had never been forthright with her about it. Whatever the reason, now she had suddenly had a bit of a shock, and her expectations of the future were suddenly drastically different.

I wish that had been the whole truth, but there was still more bad news for her.

"You know," I told her, "the problem is, it's not just the loss of the pension. It's actually worse than that because you don't get to keep both of the Social Security checks. At his death, you would only keep your Social Security payment. So, you would essentially go from $6,000 of monthly income to $1,000 of monthly income."

She got really upset at that, but I wasn't too worried at that point, because I had a solution for her. I told her, "You know, would it help you to know that I happen to be an expert at fixing problems like this? If you'd allow me, I can fix this problem for you."

That made difference. She recovered a bit, and although I could tell I wasn't the minister's best friend anymore, I'd certainly become her best friend.

"Yes," she said to me, "If you can solve this, we really want to see how to do it."

So, I turned back to the minister, and I said, "Sir, knowing that I am an expert at solving these kind of problems, would you allow me an opportunity to show you what we can do to fix this?"

Well, what do you think his answer was?

He was very polite about it, but he very firmly said, "No."

"No?" his wife said, "What do you mean, no?"

"I've already got it taken care of."

Well, that's a load off my mind. Remember, these aren't my clients, this is just a nice couple who wanted a little advice. I was running late for other appointments. I was ready to go home. If they had a great plan already, I was happy for them.

I told him as much. I said, "That's great news because I could tell your wife was getting pretty concerned there for a minute. Since you've taken care of it, would you mind sharing with us what your plan is, just for her peace of mind?"

For the first time in a few minutes, he perked up. "Sure, I'd be happy to," he said, turning to his wife, "You know, if I don't survive you, you can just marry a deacon in the church."

I suppose he thought he was being generous by letting her have her pick of the deacons. She clearly didn't see it that way, but he was satisfied that he'd solved the problem.

I tried a few more times to get him to listen to reason, but he was confident he had it figured out. Of course, it wasn't really much of a plan, but I can only help people when everybody involved cares. I told you before, I'm not much of a salesman. If both spouses aren't truly invested in getting their finances right, there's not much I can do.

The truth is, unfortunately, that many people simply don't care enough about what happens after they depart this world to plan for those they are leaving behind. They think their little schemes will be enough to get everyone by, and they want to leave it at that. They don't want to accept that only two things are certain in life, and that it's their duty to prepare for both.

I can't do anything for those people, but I can do plenty for you. That is, if you care for your family, and you want to keep taking care of them after you're gone. In that case, there's a lot we can do together to make that happen.

Here's a happier story for you. This one is about another couple, their names are Sally and Tom. They are a loving couple if ever there was one. They'd been together 55 years when I met them, and they were still crazy about each other. They held hands the whole time in my office. It's wonderful to see that sort of thing, isn't it?

So, Tom's and Sally's situation was not so different from the minister and his wife above. Tom received $1,400 a month in

Social Security, while Sally received $500. Tom also got a pension of about $2,000 a month. The problem for them was almost exactly the same: if Sally outlived Tom, she'd watch her income go from $3,900 a month to $2,400 a month.

Why is that? Well, the loss of $1,500 a month is based on Sally losing 50% of Tom's pension (he didn't take his full pension, so she would lose about $1,000 instead of the full $2,000), and the smaller of the two social security checks (the other $500 missing). Just so you don't have to do the math, that means $18,000 a year.

A quick word on pensions, in case you're confused. Pension payout options vary. In the case of the minister, when he took his full pension, there was nothing left for his wife. Here, if Tom dies first, Sally will receive half of the original monthly payout. It's important for you to find out exactly what happens with your and your spouse's pension. You don't want to get the same nasty surprise the minister's wife did. Thankfully, that's one of the many things we can work through together.

Back to Tom and Sally. In 10 years, Sally would lose $180,000 of income if they didn't do anything. That was pretty tough news to Sally, especially since those ten years are the years she's most likely to need that extra income.

After coming to see me about this, Sally and Tom agreed that they wanted to do whatever it took to make sure Sally's income would be approximately the same as it is now.

Once we had sorted through our options and come up with the right solution for them, I encouraged Tom to write Sally a letter about the whole experience, which I could put in this book.

So, please read Tom's letter, and while you do so, ask yourself: How would you feel if your spouse did this for you?

Dear Sally,

Sweetheart, I'm writing this letter to let you know that Philip and I have figured out how to solve those financial concerns we've been talking about. As you know, our pension and Social Security income is $3,900 per month. That's plenty for us. I think we live well on it, and I'm happy we're enjoying our retirement with it so much.

There is that nagging concern, though, you know what I am talking about. It's hard to discuss, but I want to put it out there straight: if I go first, that means you'll be $1,500 short every month for the rest of your life.

I just can't live with that. My goal has always been to provide enough for you so you never have to struggle, and that includes after I'm gone. In order to achieve that goal, Philip convinced me that I should purchase a life insurance policy which will provide you with a $300,000 death benefit. That money is going to be income and estate tax free.

The income from this new life insurance policy should replace the income you stand to lose, and that includes if your health turns poorly later on in life. The policy contains provisions that can assist with the cost of long-term care.

So, you see, Sally, my love, this policy is exactly what we were looking for. It protects you in the future, and it gives me peace of mind now.

Even about that, let's get back to having all that retirement fun.

Lots of Love,

Tom

Now, tell me, how would you feel if your spouse wrote a letter like that? Pretty good, right? Tell me something else, what kind of letter is Tom writing to Sally at this point?

Maybe that's a little tough to gauge with all the numbers and accounting language in there, but let me simplify it for you: this is a love letter. Isn't this letter screaming out, "I love you and I want to take care of you?"

Unlike the minister above, Tom understood there was a problem. There's going to be a shortfall of about $18,000 a year that he needed to make up for in order to help his wife, and he made the smart choice to resolve that through the purchase of life insurance. What that shows, more than anything, is that he wanted to make the effort, that he cared, and when both Sally and Tom care, then I can step in and do what needs to be done to make this happen.

When both parties care, and both parties are willing to see the problems ahead, that's when I can step in and make a difference. I'm a fixer, but I can only fix things when everyone admits they're broken.

That's how my job works. I'm like a driver out on a road late at night. It's foggy and rainy, and it's hard to see. So, I stop on the side of the road because I've found out that something's wrong with the road ahead. I get a good look from atop a little hill, and I can see that the bridge has been washed away. At that point, my job is clear. When I see you coming down the road behind me, I don't just stand there and let you go over the edge. I race out into the road and hold up my arms and scream, "Hey, you need to stop here, and let's fix this problem so that you don't have some negative consequences."

Of course, it's entirely up to you whether you stop and listen to the guy waving his arms in the road or if you drive around him and continue on. But if you do stop, then I know we can find a solution to that problem. We can find another way across that river together. But we can only do that if you stop.

That's how I see what I do. I'm here to protect people from an inevitable crash, and I have an opportunity to step in and change that course of events. I'll keep waving my arms and screaming, all you have to do is slow down and listen to what I have to tell you.

But how am I going to help you? What's the big secret that allows me to help people like Tom and Sally, or that would have let me help the minister and his wife? We learned one strategy in the last chapter, which was the indexed annuity that could protect you from one kind of money loss: the risks of the market. But that strategy wouldn't be enough for Tom and Sally, or for the minister and his wife. For them, we need something more.

To find that solution, we have to go back to those two inevitable facts in life: death and taxes. I can't change the death part, so that leaves taxes.

Here's the thing about taxes: they're written by a certain group of people with certain priorities. So, tell me, who writes this tax code? I know a lot of your will say it's the IRS, but the IRS doesn't write the rules, it just enforces them. So, who actually writes the laws?

Congress, of course. And what do we know about people in Congress? They're liars, sure. They're greedy, certainly. They're corrupt, that's probably true as well. What else?

They're rich. If they're not millionaires before they get in to office, they're certainly millionaires when they get out. And millionaires need to use this tax code to transfer wealth from one generation to the next. That's one of the big goals of having money: passing it down. These are the guys who write the laws, and these are the guys who want to hold on to their money, so what are they going to do? Make sure they can keep it all.

How do they do it? Two words: life insurance.

That's how Tom made sure Sally would be taken care of, and that's how the minister could have taken care of his wife. That's also how you can make sure your spouse and your family are taken care of after you're gone.

So, for the next couple chapters, I want to talk to you about how to make your money last by avoiding the taxman. And, it all comes down to life insurance.

The trick to passing on your savings really comes down to how to turn taxable income into tax-free income. This is a tax code that is highly prized by wealthy people, and it's been around a long time. No matter what gets passed in Congress this year or next year or ten years from now, it will survive every change. This particular item will not see any revisions because it's a way that rich people (i.e. Congresspeople) are able to transfer their wealth without taxes.

The thing is, they haven't written a special exception for themselves in there. We get to use the same tax code they do. In fact, they've written it all out in plain enough English, it's just they hide it deep in the tax documents.

Take a look at Form 525, for instance. If you look at the next page, you can see that life insurance gets preferential treatment here.

Department of the Treasury
Internal Revenue Service

Publication 525
Cat. No. 15047D

Taxable and Nontaxable Income

For use in preparing
2016 Returns

Get forms and other information faster and easier at:
- *IRS.gov* (English)
- *IRS.gov/Korean* (한국어)
- *IRS.gov/Spanish* (Español)
- *IRS.gov/Russian* (Pусский)
- *IRS.gov/Chinese* (中文)
- *IRS.gov/Vietnamese* (TiếngViệt)

Jan 23, 2017

Contents

Future Developments

For the latest information about developments related to Publication 525, such as legislation enacted after it was published, go to *www.irs.gov/pub525*.

What's New

Olympic and Paralympic medals and United States Olympic Committee (USOC) prize money. If you receive Olympic and Paralympic medals and USOC prize money, the value of the medals and the amount of the prize money may be non-taxable. See the instructions for line 21, Form 1040, at *www.irs.gov/pub/irs-pdf/i1040.pdf* for more information.

Health flexible spending arrangements (health FSAs) under cafeteria plans. For tax years beginning in 2016, the dollar limitation under section 125(i) on voluntary employee salary reductions for contributions to health flexible spending arrangements is $2,550.

Reminders

Achieving a Better Life Experience (ABLE) account. This is a new type of savings account for individuals with disabilities and their families. Distributions are tax-free if used to pay the beneficiary's qualified disability expenses. See Pub. 907 for more information.

Public safety officers. A spouse, former spouse, and child of a public safety officer killed in the line of duty can exclude from gross income survivor benefits received from a governmental section 401(a) plan attributable to the officer's service. See section 101(h).

A public safety officer that's permanently and totally disabled or killed in the line of duty

Excluded debt. Do not include a canceled debt in your gross income in the following situations.

- The debt is canceled in a bankruptcy case under Title 11 of the U.S. Code. See Pub. 908.
- The debt is canceled when you are insolvent. However, you can't exclude any amount of canceled debt that is more than the amount by which you are insolvent. See Pub. 908.
- The debt is qualified farm debt and is canceled by a qualified person. See chapter 3 of Pub. 225.
- The debt is qualified real property business debt. See chapter 5 of Pub. 334.
- The cancellation is intended as a gift.
- The debt is qualified principal residence indebtedness, discussed next.

Qualified principal residence indebtedness (QPRI). This is debt secured by your principal residence that you took out to buy, build, or substantially improve your principal residence. QPRI can't be more than the cost of your principal residence plus improvements.

You must reduce the basis of your principal residence by the amount excluded from gross income. To claim the exclusion, you must file Form 982 with your tax return.

Principal residence. Your principal residence is the home where you ordinarily live most of the time. You can have only one principal residence at any one time.

Amount eligible for exclusion. The maximum amount you can treat as QPRI is $2 million ($1 million if married filing separately). You can't exclude debt canceled because of services performed for the lender or on account of any other factor not directly related to a decline in the value of your residence or to your financial condition.

Limitation. If only part of a loan is QPRI, the exclusion applies only to the extent the canceled amount is more than the amount of the loan immediately before the cancellation that isn't QPRI.

Example. Your principal residence is secured by a debt of $1 million, of which $800,000 is QPRI. Your residence is sold for $700,000 and $300,000 of debt is canceled. $100,000 of the canceled debt may be excluded from income (the $300,000 canceled debt is discharged minus the $200,000 of nonqualified debt).

Host or Hostess

If you host a party or event at which sales are made, any gift or gratuity you receive for giving the event is a payment for helping a direct seller make sales. You must report this item as income at its fair market value.

Your out-of-pocket party expenses are subject to the 50% limit for meal and entertainment expenses. These expenses are deductible as miscellaneous itemized deductions subject to the 2%-of-AGI limit on Schedule A (Form 1040), but only up to the amount of income you receive for giving the party.

For more information about the 50% limit for meal and entertainment expenses, see *50% Limit* in Pub. 463.

Life Insurance Proceeds

Life insurance proceeds paid to you because of the death of the insured person aren't taxable unless the policy was turned over to you for a price. This is true even if the proceeds were paid under an accident or health insurance policy or an endowment contract. However, interest income received as a result of life insurance proceeds may be taxable.

Proceeds not received in installments. If death benefits are paid to you in a lump sum or other than at regular intervals, include in your income only the benefits that are more than the amount payable to you at the time of the insured person's death. If the benefit payable at death isn't specified, you include in your income the benefit payments that are more than the present value of the payments at the time of death.

Proceeds received in installments. If you receive life insurance proceeds in installments, you can exclude part of each installment from your income.

To determine the excluded part, divide the amount held by the insurance company (generally the total lump sum payable at the death of the insured person) by the number of installments to be paid. Include anything over this excluded part in your income as interest.

Example. The face amount of the policy is $75,000 and, as beneficiary, you choose to receive 120 monthly installments of $1,000 each. The excluded part of each installment is $625 ($75,000 ÷ 120), or $7,500 for an entire year. The rest of each payment, $375 a month (or $4,500 for an entire year), is interest income to you.

Installments for life. If, as the beneficiary under an insurance contract, you are entitled to receive the proceeds in installments for the rest of your life without a refund or period-certain guarantee, you figure the excluded part of each installment by dividing the amount held by the insurance company by your life expectancy. If there is a refund or period-certain guarantee, the amount held by the insurance company for this purpose is reduced by the actuarial value of the guarantee.

Surviving spouse. If your spouse died before October 23, 1986, and insurance proceeds paid to you because of the death of your spouse are received in installments, you can exclude up to $1,000 a year of the interest included in the installments. If you remarry, you can continue to take the exclusion.

Employer-owned life insurance contract. If you are the policyholder of an employer-owned life insurance contract, you must include in income any life insurance proceeds received that are more than the premiums and any other amounts you paid on the policy. You are subject to this rule if you have a trade or business, you own a life insurance contract on the life of your

employee, and you (or a related person) are a beneficiary under the contract.

However, you may exclude the full amount of the life insurance proceeds if the following apply.

1. Before the policy is issued, you provide written notice about the insurance to the employee and the employee provides written consent to be insured.
2. Either:
   a. The employee was your employee within the 12-month period before death, or, at the time the contract was issued, was a director or highly compensated employee, or
   b. The amount is paid to the family or designated beneficiary of the employee.

Interest option on insurance. If an insurance company pays you interest only on proceeds from life insurance left on deposit, the interest you are paid is taxable.

If your spouse died before October 23, 1986, and you chose to receive only the interest from your insurance proceeds, the $1,000 interest exclusion for a surviving spouse doesn't apply. If you later decide to receive the proceeds from the policy in installments, you can take the interest exclusion from the time you begin to receive the installments.

Surrender of policy for cash. If you surrender a life insurance policy for cash, you must include in income any proceeds that are more than the cost of the life insurance policy. In most cases, your cost (or investment in the contract) is the total of premiums that you paid for the life insurance policy, less any refunded premiums, rebates, dividends, or unrepaid loans that were not included in your income.

You should receive a Form 1099-R showing the total proceeds and the taxable part. Report these amounts on lines 16a and 16b of Form 1040 or on lines 12a and 12b of Form 1040A.

 For information on when the proceeds are excluded from income, see Accelerated Death Benefits, later.

Split-dollar life insurance. In most cases, a split-dollar life insurance arrangement is an arrangement between an owner and a non-owner of a life insurance contract under which either party to the arrangement pays all or part of the premiums, and one of the parties paying the premiums is entitled to recover all or part of those premiums from the proceeds of the contract. There are two mutually exclusive rules to tax split-dollar life insurance arrangements.

1. Under the economic benefit rule, the owner of the life insurance contract is treated as providing current life insurance protection and other taxable economic benefits to the non-owner of the contract.
2. Under the loan rule, the non-owner of the life insurance contract is treated as loaning premium payments to the owner of the contract.

Only one of these regimes applies to any one policy. For more information, see sections 1.61-22 and 1.7872-15 of the regulations.

Endowment Contract Proceeds

An endowment contract is a policy under which you are paid a specified amount of money on a certain date unless you die before that date, in which case, the money is paid to your designated beneficiary. Endowment proceeds paid in a lump-sum to you at maturity are taxable only if the proceeds are more than the cost (investment in the contract) of the policy. To determine your cost, subtract any amount that you previously received under the contract and excluded from your income from the total premiums (or other consideration) paid for the contract. Include the part of the lump-sum payment that is more than your cost in your income.

Endowment proceeds that you choose to receive in installments instead of a lump-sum payment at the maturity of the policy are taxed as an annuity. This is explained in Pub. 575. For this treatment to apply, you must choose to receive the proceeds in installments before receiving any part of the lump sum. This election must be made within 60 days after the lump-sum payment first becomes payable to you.

Accelerated Death Benefits

Certain amounts paid as accelerated death benefits under a life insurance contract or viatical settlement before the insured's death are excluded from income if the insured is terminally or chronically ill.

Viatical settlement. This is the sale or assignment of any part of the death benefit under a life insurance contract to a viatical settlement provider. A viatical settlement provider is a person who regularly engages in the business of buying or taking assignment of life insurance contracts on the lives of insured individuals who are terminally or chronically ill and who meets the requirements of section 101(g)(2)(B) of the Internal Revenue Code.

Exclusion for terminal illness. Accelerated death benefits are fully excludable if the insured is a terminally ill individual. This is a person who has been certified by a physician as having an illness or physical condition that can reasonably be expected to result in death within 24 months from the date of the certification.

Exclusion for chronic illness. If the insured is a chronically ill individual who isn't terminally ill, accelerated death benefits paid on the basis of costs incurred for qualified long-term care services are fully excludable. Accelerated death benefits paid on a *per diem* or other periodic basis are excludable up to a limit. This limit applies to the total of the accelerated death benefits and any periodic payments received from long-term care insurance contracts. For information on the limit and the definitions of chronically ill individual, qualified long-term care services, and long-term care insurance contracts,

see *Long-Term Care Insurance Contracts* under *Sickness and Injury Benefits*, earlier.

Exception. The exclusion doesn't apply to any amount paid to a person (other than the insured) who has an insurable interest in the life of the insured because the insured:

- Is a director, officer, or employee of the person, or
- Has a financial interest in the person's business.

Form 8853. To claim an exclusion for accelerated death benefits made on a *per diem* or other periodic basis, you must file Form 8853 with your return. You don't have to file Form 8853 to exclude accelerated death benefits paid on the basis of actual expenses incurred.

Recoveries

A recovery is a return of an amount you deducted or took a credit for in an earlier year. The most common recoveries are refunds, reimbursements, and rebates of itemized deductions. You also may have recoveries of non-itemized deductions (such as payments on previously deducted bad debts) and recoveries of items for which you previously claimed a tax credit.

Tax benefit rule. You must include a recovery in your income in the year you receive it up to the amount by which the deduction or credit you took for the recovered amount reduced your tax in the earlier year. For this purpose, any increase to an amount carried over to the current year that resulted from the deduction or credit is considered to have reduced your tax in the earlier year.

Federal income tax refund. Refunds of federal income taxes aren't included in your income because they are never allowed as a deduction from income.

State tax refund. If you received a state or local income tax refund (or credit or offset) in 2016, you generally must include it in income if you deducted the tax in an earlier year. The payer should send Form 1099-G, to you by February 1, 2017. The IRS also will receive a copy of the Form 1099-G. If you file Form 1040, use the worksheet in the 2016 Form 1040 instructions for line 10 to figure the amount (if any) to include in your income. See *Itemized Deduction Recoveries*, later, for when you must use *Worksheet 2*, later in this publication.

If you could choose to deduct for a tax year either:

- State and local income taxes, or
- State and local general sales taxes, then

the maximum refund that you may have to include in income is limited to the excess of the tax you chose to deduct for that year over the tax you didn't choose to deduct for that year.

Example 1. For 2015 you can choose an $11,000 state income tax deduction or a $10,000 state general sales tax deduction. You choose to deduct the state income tax. In 2016 you receive a $2,500 state income tax refund.

The maximum refund that you may have to include in income is $1,000, since you could have deducted $10,000 in state general sales tax.

Example 2. For 2015 you can choose an $11,500 state general sales tax deduction based on actual expenses or an $11,200 state income tax deduction. You choose to deduct the general sales tax deduction. In 2016 you return an item that you had purchased and receive a $500 sales tax refund. In 2016 you also receive a $1,500 state income tax refund. The maximum refund that you may have to include in income is $500, since it is less than the excess of the tax deducted ($11,500) over the tax you didn't choose to deduct ($11,200 − $1,500 = $9,700). Since you didn't choose to deduct the state income tax, you don't include the state income tax refund in income.

Mortgage interest refund. If you received a refund or credit in 2016 of mortgage interest paid in an earlier year, the amount should be shown in box 3 of your Form 1098. Do not subtract the refund amount from the interest you paid in 2016. You may have to include it in your income under the rules explained in the following discussions.

Interest on recovery. Interest on any of the amounts you recover must be reported as interest income in the year received. For example, report any interest you received on state or local income tax refunds on Form 1040, line 8a or Form 1040NR, line 9a.

Recovery and expense in same year. If the refund or other recovery and the expense occur in the same year, the recovery reduces the deduction or credit and isn't reported as income.

Recovery for 2 or more years. If you receive a refund or other recovery that is for amounts you paid in 2 or more separate years, you must allocate, on a *pro rata* basis, the recovered amount between the years in which you paid it. This allocation is necessary to determine the amount of recovery from any earlier years and to determine the amount, if any, of your allowable deduction for this item for the current year.

Example. You paid 2015 estimated state income tax of $4,000 in four equal payments. You made your fourth payment in January 2016. You had no state income tax withheld during 2015. In 2016, you received a $400 tax refund based on your 2015 state income tax return. You claimed itemized deductions each year on Schedule A (Form 1040).

You must allocate the $400 refund between 2015 and 2016, the years in which you paid the tax on which the refund is based. You paid 75% ($3,000 ÷ $4,000) of the estimated tax in 2015, so 75% of the $400 refund, or $300, is for amounts you paid in 2015 and is a recovery item. If all of the $300 is a taxable recovery item, you will include $300 on Form 1040, line 10, for 2016, and attach a copy of your computation showing why that amount is less than the amount shown on the Form 1099-G you received from the state.

The balance ($100) of the $400 refund is for your January 2016 estimated tax payment. When you figure your deduction for state and

Publication 525 (2016)

The form says that life insurance, when you inherit it, is completely income tax free, inheritance tax free, probate free. If you look at the next page after that, you can see that life insurance can do more than that. It allows you to draw from this death benefit and use it as a living benefit, either for terminal illness or for custodial care, or for nursing care. We'll talk more about this in Chapter 5, but all that's important at this point is recognizing this fact: with life insurance, it's like you've got a large stack of checks that are going to pass directly to your heirs without taxes, and if you need it during your lifetime, you have another checkbook that you can draw from to pay for care in your home or care in a facility or care in a nursing home.

Now, I'm not saying there are not other ways to save and make money, the problem is, there aren't others ways to do that and to avoid paying a big chunk in taxes. If you stick with your plan—whatever it is now—your family is going to be writing checks to the IRS, we'll just make them payable now, you can sign them for about a third of whatever you have in your IRA account. Or, you can use my plan that allows the family to get the money instead. You can write all those checks and still not shortchange the IRS. How is that? Well, let's go back to our five buckets.

Remember the farmer and the IRS agent? We're going to learn from his example, and we're going to use the **5% Solution** to solve this problem. Basically, we're just going to take some of the money from your Never Bucket—that 5%—and we're going to pay some tax on that right now, then we're going to put it in life insurance and put all that life insurance money into the tax-free Harvest Bucket. We're just going to reap the harvest of that 5% of your money that you were never planning to spend anyway. That's where you get the real benefit from in your financial life. It's that simple. That is the end of the story.

One final word on this benefit. If you have a life insurance plan already, you may think you can forget about all of what I just told you. "No thanks, Philip, I already have that side of things covered."

If you do, great, but I recommend you get your policy reviewed. It's true what I said, that these benefits won't ever go away, but some benefits get added all the time. In fact, all these benefits are a function of recent life insurance policy changes. If you bought your policy some years ago, make sure that you have the latest features included. If your policy is more than seven or eight years old, for instance, you may not have the acceleration benefits included. That's what allows you to draw that money out tax free if you need it. That's going to be important, so you want to make sure you have it, or else you want to get it added quickly.

The great news is that most of these things can be added in without any cost to you. They're just included in the policy itself. I can check that out for you and make the changes very quickly and painlessly.

I'm thankful that another of my clients, Betty, listened to me when I called out a warning about her finances. She had a $100,000 annuity, and she'd had it a long time. Like a lot of people, she just took her statements when she got them in the mail and filed them away without ever really paying any attention to them.

Without really knowing it, over the last ten years, like the rest of my clients, she'd managed to double the account to be worth about $200,000. She thought that was great news when I told her, but less great was when she found out that with an annuity, the money is tax deferred, but it's not tax free.

So, someday, somebody is going to have to pay the taxes on that $100,000 gain. Either Betty herself is going to have to pay it when she draws it out, or when she passes, her heirs will have to pay it. Again, we're not talking about change here, we're looking at about a $30,000 hit for Betty or her heirs.

Betty was understandably upset to receive that news. Because she's been around a while, she remembered her first job where she earned 75 cents an hour. She's a woman who knows how hard it is to save anything at all; she remembered how hard she had to work to scrimp and save her first $30,000. She didn't want to make her family pay all that money. She was counting on giving that to her family, and she wanted her family to take full advantage of having that money instead of it going to the IRS.

$30,000 might pay for her granddaughter's first year of college; it might mean the difference between her going to the school of her dreams and deciding not to go at all.

Once she understood this, she was understandably concerned, but I had a way to help her. I told her that I had a way to assist her by transitioning her money, just like I'm showing you here. First, I pulled out another tax form, Form 575, which you can see on the next page. Form 575 applies to all annuities, and I showed her what her annuity meant both for her and for her granddaughter.

The good thing, I told her, was the form said that her earnings wouldn't be taxed until distributed. The bad thing, however, is that the interest comes out first. So, if Betty wanted to pay for that first year of her granddaughter's college while she was still alive, and that first year cost $50,000, that $50,000 would come from the interest, and would get taxed as income. That would be true if she drew the money out during her lifetime. She'd be paying taxes on it until she got down to her base, that initial $100,000.

You can see the details of that right on the second page of 575, where the page is highlighted.

I then explained how the third page of 575 explains what happens for inheritors. Say Betty didn't touch a cent in her annuity. Well, according to the form, whoever inherits the money has to pay the income taxes on the gain, which is that extra $100,000 she'd earned on the annuity up to that point. But it wouldn't be just that simple. First of all, the tax would be due all at once. Also, in Pennsylvania, her inheritors would pay inheritance tax on the whole $200,000, as well as that income tax on the $100,000 in interest. So, when I told her it would $30,000, I was really low balling her on what will be due. With the tax due to Pennsylvania, it really adds up to about 40% lost to taxes.

Department of the Treasury
Internal Revenue Service

Publication 575
Cat. No. 15142B

Pension and Annuity Income

For use in preparing

2016 Returns

Get forms and other information faster and easier at:
- *IRS.gov* (English)
- *IRS.gov/Spanish* (Español)
- *IRS.gov/Chinese* (中文)
- *IRS.gov/Korean* (한국어)
- *IRS.gov/Russian* (Русский)
- *IRS.gov/Vietnamese* (TiếngViệt)

Contents

Reminders

Future developments. For the latest information about developments related to Pub. 575, such as legislation enacted after it was published, go to *www.irs.gov/pub575*.

Net investment income tax. For purposes of the net investment income tax (NIIT), net investment income doesn't include distributions from a qualified retirement plan (for example, 401(a), 403(a), 403(b), 408, 408A, or 457(b) plans). However, these distributions are taken into account when determining the modified adjusted gross income threshold. Distributions from a nonqualified retirement plan are included in net investment income. See Form 8960, Net Investment Income Tax - Individuals, Estates, and Trusts, and its instructions for more information.

Expanded exception to the tax on early distributions from a governmental plan for qualified public safety employees. For tax years beginning after December 31, for an employee under a plan that meets Internal Revenue Code requirements.

Designated Roth account. A designated Roth account is a separate account created under a qualified Roth contribution program to which participants may elect to have part or all of their elective deferrals to a 401(k), 403(b), or 457(b) plan designated as Roth contributions. Elective deferrals that are designated as Roth contributions are included in your income. However, qualified distributions (explained later) aren't included in your income. You should check with your plan administrator to determine if your plan will accept designated Roth contributions.

Tax-sheltered annuity plan. A tax-sheltered annuity plan (often referred to as a 403(b) plan or a tax-deferred annuity plan) is a retirement plan for employees of public schools and certain tax-exempt organizations. Generally, a tax-sheltered annuity plan provides retirement benefits by purchasing annuity contracts for its participants.

Types of pensions and annuities. Pensions and annuities include the following types.

Fixed-period annuities. You receive definite amounts at regular intervals for a specified length of time.

Annuities for a single life. You receive definite amounts at regular intervals for life. The payments end at death.

Joint and survivor annuities. The first annuitant receives a definite amount at regular intervals for life. After he or she dies, a second annuitant receives a definite amount at regular intervals for life. The amount paid to the second annuitant may or may not differ from the amount paid to the first annuitant.

Variable annuities. You receive payments that may vary in amount for a specified length of time or for life. The amounts you receive may depend upon such variables as profits earned by the pension or annuity funds, cost-of-living indexes, or earnings from a mutual fund.

Disability pensions. You receive disability payments because you retired on disability and haven't reached minimum retirement age.

More than one program. You may receive employee plan benefits from more than one program under a single trust or plan of your employer. If you participate in more than one program, you may have to treat each as a separate pension or annuity contract, depending upon the facts in each case. Also, you may be considered to have received more than one pension or annuity. Your former employer or the plan administrator should be able to tell you if you have more than one contract.

Example. Your employer set up a noncontributory profit-sharing plan for its employees. The plan provides that the amount held in the account of each participant will be paid when that participant retires. Your employer also set up a contributory defined benefit pension plan for its

employees providing for the payment of a lifetime pension to each participant after retirement.

The amount of any distribution from the profit-sharing plan depends on the contributions (including allocated forfeitures) made for the participant and the earnings from those contributions. Under the pension plan, however, a formula determines the amount of the pension benefits. The amount of contributions is the amount necessary to provide that pension.

Each plan is a separate program and a separate contract. If you get benefits from these plans, you must account for each separately, even though the benefits from both may be included in the same check.

 Distributions from a designated Roth account are treated separately from other distributions from the plan.

Qualified domestic relations order (QDRO). A QDRO is a judgment, decree, or order relating to payment of child support, alimony, or marital property rights to a spouse, former spouse, child, or other dependent of a participant in a retirement plan. The QDRO must contain certain specific information, such as the name and last known mailing address of the participant and each alternate payee, and the amount or percentage of the participant's benefits to be paid to each alternate payee. A QDRO may not award an amount or form of benefit that isn't available under the plan.

A spouse or former spouse who receives part of the benefits from a retirement plan under a QDRO reports the payments received as if he or she were a plan participant. The spouse or former spouse is allocated a share of the participant's cost (investment in the contract) equal to the cost times a fraction. The numerator of the fraction is the present value of the benefits payable to the spouse or former spouse. The denominator is the present value of all benefits payable to the participant.

A distribution that is paid to a child or other dependent under a QDRO is taxed to the plan participant.

Variable Annuities

The tax rules in this publication apply both to annuities that provide fixed payments and to annuities that provide payments that vary in amount based on investment results or other factors. For example, they apply to commercial variable annuity contracts, whether bought by an employee retirement plan for its participants or bought directly from the issuer by an individual investor. Under these contracts, the owner can generally allocate the purchase payments among several types of investment portfolios or mutual funds and the contract value is determined by the performance of those investments. The earnings aren't taxed until distributed either in a withdrawal or in annuity payments. The taxable part of a distribution is treated as ordinary income.

For information on the tax treatment of a transfer or exchange of a variable annuity contract, see *Transfers of Annuity Contracts* under *Taxation of Nonperiodic Payments,* later.

Net investment income tax. Annuities under a nonqualified plan are included in calculating your net investment income for the net investment income tax (NIIT). For information see the Instructions for Form 8960, Net Investment Income Tax — Individuals, Estates and Trusts.

Withdrawals. If you withdraw funds before your annuity starting date and your annuity is under a qualified retirement plan, a ratable part of the amount withdrawn is tax free. The tax-free part is based on the ratio of your cost (investment in the contract) to your account balance under the plan.

If your annuity is under a nonqualified plan (including a contract you bought directly from the issuer), the amount withdrawn is allocated first to earnings (the taxable part) and then to your cost (the tax-free part). However, if you bought your annuity contract before August 14, 1982, a different allocation applies to the investment before that date and the earnings on that investment. To the extent the amount withdrawn doesn't exceed that investment and earnings, it is allocated first to your cost (the tax-free part) and then to earnings (the taxable part).

If you withdraw funds (other than as an annuity) on or after your annuity starting date, the entire amount withdrawn is generally taxable.

The amount you receive in a full surrender of your annuity contract at any time is tax free to the extent of any cost that you haven't previously recovered tax free. The rest is taxable.

For more information on the tax treatment of withdrawals, see _Taxation of Nonperiodic Payments_, later. If you withdraw funds from your annuity before you reach age 59 ½, also see _Tax on Early Distributions_ under _Special Additional Taxes_, later.

Annuity payments. If you receive annuity payments under a variable annuity plan or contract, you recover your cost tax free under either the Simplified Method or the General Rule, as explained under _Taxation of Periodic Payments_, later. For a variable annuity paid under a qualified plan, you generally must use the Simplified Method. For a variable annuity paid under a nonqualified plan (including a contract you bought directly from the issuer), you must use a special computation under the General Rule. For more information, see _Variable annuities_ in Pub. 939 under _Computation Under the General Rule_.

Death benefits. If you receive a single-sum distribution from a variable annuity contract because of the death of the owner or annuitant, the distribution is generally taxable only to the extent it is more than the unrecovered cost of the contract. If you choose to receive an annuity, the payments are subject to tax as described above. If the contract provides a joint and survivor annuity and the primary annuitant had received annuity payments before death, you figure the tax-free part of annuity payments you receive as the survivor in the same way the primary annuitant did. See _Survivors and Beneficiaries_, later.

Section 457 Deferred Compensation Plans

If you work for a state or local government or for a tax-exempt organization, you may be able to participate in a section 457 deferred compensation plan. If your plan is an eligible plan, you aren't taxed currently on pay that is deferred under the plan or on any earnings from the plan's investment of the deferred pay. You are generally taxed on amounts deferred in an eligible state or local government plan only when they are distributed from the plan. You are taxed on amounts deferred in an eligible tax-exempt organization plan when they are distributed or otherwise made available to you.

Your 457(b) plan may have a designated Roth account option. If so, you may be able to roll over amounts to the designated Roth account or make contributions. Elective deferrals to a designated Roth account are included in your income. Qualified distributions (explained later) aren't included in your income. See the _Designated Roth accounts_ discussion under _Taxation of Periodic Payments_, later.

This publication covers the tax treatment of benefits under eligible section 457 plans, but it doesn't cover the treatment of deferrals. For information on deferrals under section 457 plans, see _Retirement Plan Contributions_ under _Employee Compensation_ in Pub. 525.

Is your plan eligible? To find out if your plan is an eligible plan, check with your employer. Plans that aren't eligible section 457 plans include the following:

- Bona fide vacation leave, sick leave, compensatory time, severance pay, disability pay, or death benefit plans.

- Nonelective deferred compensation plans for nonemployees (independent contractors).

- Deferred compensation plans maintained by churches.

- Length of service award plans for bona fide volunteer firefighters and emergency medical personnel. An exception applies if the total amount paid to a volunteer exceeds $3,000 for any year of service.

Disability Pensions

If you retired on disability, you generally must include in income any disability pension you receive under a plan that is paid for by your employer. You must report your taxable disability payments as wages on line 7 of Form 1040 or Form 1040A or on line 8 of Form 1040NR until you reach minimum retirement age. Minimum retirement age generally is the age at which you can first receive a pension or annuity if you aren't disabled.

 You may be entitled to a tax credit if you were permanently and totally disabled when you retired. For information on this credit, see Pub. 524.

Beginning on the day after you reach minimum retirement age, payments you receive are taxable as a pension

At this point, she was heading past upset and moving on to devastated.

"What am I supposed to do?"

She seemed to think that money was just gone. All that hard work to save that money, and her granddaughter was going to lose almost half of it.

Well, I told her, there's plenty we can do. First, she was smart to put her money in an annuity. In an IRA, every penny is taxable. In a non-qualified annuity like hers, only the gain is taxable, but whether her money was in an annuity or an IRA or just under her mattress, the same solution would apply. Once again, we would use the **5% Solution**: we'd take 5% from her annuity, pay the tax on it now, and we'd use that seed money to create a completely tax-free, probate-free, inheritance tax-free life insurance benefit that replaces almost the entire account of the annuity, all while leaving the remaining annuity balance basically untouched. With the **5% Solution**, we were able to buy more than enough life insurance to offset the cost of the taxes that it would be lost to the family and provide a whole lot more in additional funds that she would be able to leave to her family than just the annuity alone after taxes.

As you can imagine, Betty was pretty grateful about this discovery. Not only would she be able to leave the money for her granddaughter to go to her preferred college for the first year, she'd be able to finance the entire four-year degree.

Because she was so overjoyed, I asked her to write a letter just like Tom did to tell her granddaughter the good news.

Dear Katie,

I am writing this letter to let you know I've been worried for a while. You're too young to have these kinds of financial worries, but I want to explain them to you now just so you know how much I care.

I currently have approximately $200,000 in my annuities, which I have been hoping would go to you to help you go to your dream college, wherever that is. I know that sounds like a lot, but the reason I've been worried is that 100% of the interest in the annuities, which is half the value, is subject to income taxes. That means the IRS would take as much as $40,000 of that money. If any of the money gets used before that or for other purposes... well, you can see how quickly your college fund would disappear.

But don't worry, my dear. I fixed the whole problem. All I had to do was purchase a life insurance policy. I've been working with a very nice financial advisor who taught me all the secrets to make sure you get the start to life you deserve. Now, because of this life insurance policy, there will be a $340,000 death benefit which is generally free of income and estate taxes. That will easily cover the taxes on my annuity and leave more than enough for your schooling. I'm so overjoyed by this! You'll end up with more than double the amount of money, which means you won't have to worry about any debts early in life.

There's more, but this concerns your mother more than you. In addition to the fact there will be enough money now after I'm gone, the policy also allows me to take out money for long-term care if I need it, up to $130,000. Of course, that would reduce the amount you get, so let's hope we don't *need it, but if we do, what a relief to know I won't be a drag on you and your mother.*

So, you see my darling, this policy can be beneficial to you and to me. It means so much to me that your future, and mine, are so secure now.

Love You Always,
Grandma

Once again, let me ask you, what kind of letter is this? This is a letter of love from a grandmother to her granddaughter, showing that Grandma has taken care of everything. What a gift this is to her granddaughter Katie, not just the chance to go to any college, but the knowledge that Grandma will be taken care of for the rest of her life.

We were able to do that because Betty and I worked together to essentially double the value of her annuity by using the **5% Solution** to draw a little bit out, pay taxes on it, and put it in a tax free Harvest Bucket.

Chapter 4

Choosing Your Beneficiaries

There are few decisions in life more important than picking your beneficiaries. First of all, it's crucial you do this to make sure your assets go to the people you want, and in the proportion you want. But also, as we discovered in the last chapter with Betty and Tom, assigning beneficiaries is one of the greatest ways to show that you love someone. You are taking care of those people long after you're actually gone. How many people are capable of doing that?

Therefore, I think it's important at this point in the discussion of your finances to take a moment to slow down and thinking about who you want your beneficiaries to be. Who do you want to give that incredible gift of love and financial protection to?

In the last chapter, I introduced you to a number of former clients I've met along the way in my career. I hope those stories have helped to enrich your understanding of why you need to take the options I'm presenting here seriously.

I'd like to tell you about another client in this chapter. His name is John, and when I met John, he had all of his money in an IRA. Now, before I tell you John's story, I want to say upfront that I know a lot of you have IRAs, and I want you to know there's nothing wrong with that. I'm not on a campaign against IRAs. They can be a great way to grow your wealth, but they are just not really what you want your finances hanging on long term. At a certain point in your life—which is the point John was at a few years ago—you want something safer, something that isn't going to have any costs later down the road.

I get a lot of resistance on that point, I got some from John in fact, and the way I like to get people to rethink their understanding of an IRA is by asking one simple question: what do you think IRA stands for?

I know what you're thinking. You've probably heard it a million times, and you think I've finally given you an easy one to answer. You say it this way, your broker says it this way, people on TV say it this way too. You know the right answer: individual retirement account.

The problem is, that is 100% false. If you look at the tax code in Form 590a, if you look at that page I've included on the next page, you can see that it's "individual retirement arrangement." An IRA isn't based on accounts, it's based on an arrangement. This can be a very fruitful arrangement earlier in your life, but just so you completely understand, it's an arrangement in which the IRS has arranged to become your number one beneficiary. They're going to stand in first position and take your funds first before anybody else is going to get their distribution. So, in case you didn't add them to your IRA as a beneficiary, they've already taken the initiative and added themselves for you. What that means is that they're probably going to be your largest beneficiary. After all, they get first dibs.

Department of the Treasury
Internal Revenue Service

Publication 590-A
Cat. No. 66302J

Contributions to Individual Retirement Arrangements (IRAs)

For use in preparing

2016 Returns

Get forms and other information faster and easier at:
- *IRS.gov* (English)   • *IRS.gov/Korean* (한국어)
- *IRS.gov/Spanish* (Español)   • *IRS.gov/Russian* (Русский)
- *IRS.gov/Chinese* (中文)   • *IRS.gov/Vietnamese* (TiếngViệt)

Dec 28, 2016

Contents

What's New for 2016

Modified AGI limit for traditional IRA contributions. For 2016, if you are covered by a retirement plan at work, your deduction for contributions to a traditional IRA is reduced (phased out) if your modified AGI is:

- More than $98,000 but less than $118,000 for a married couple filing a joint return or a qualifying widow(er),

- More than $61,000 but less than $71,000 for a single individual or head of household, or

- Less than $10,000 for a married individual filing a separate return.

Modified AGI limit for certain married individuals increased. If you are married and your spouse is covered by a retirement plan at work and you are not, and you live with your spouse or file a joint return, your deduction is phased out if your modified AGI is more than $184,000 (up from $183,000 for 2015) but less than $194,000 (up from $193,000 for 2015). If your modified AGI is $194,000

What if You Inherit an IRA?

If you inherit a traditional IRA, you are called a beneficiary. A beneficiary can be any person or entity the owner chooses to receive the benefits of the IRA after he or she dies. Beneficiaries of a traditional IRA must include in their gross income any taxable distributions they receive.

Inherited from Spouse

If you inherit a traditional IRA from your spouse, you generally have the following three choices. You can:

1. Treat it as your own IRA by designating yourself as the account owner.

2. Treat it as your own by rolling it over into your IRA, or to the extent it is taxable, into a:

   a. Qualified employer plan,

   b. Qualified employee annuity plan (section 403(a) plan),

   c. Tax-sheltered annuity plan (section 403(b) plan),

   d. Deferred compensation plan of a state or local government (section 457 plan), or

3. Treat yourself as the beneficiary rather than treating the IRA as your own.

Treating it as your own. You will be considered to have chosen to treat the IRA as your own if:

- Contributions (including rollover contributions) are made to the inherited IRA, or

- You do not take the required minimum distribution for a year as a beneficiary of the IRA.

You will only be considered to have chosen to treat the IRA as your own if:

- You are the sole beneficiary of the IRA, and

- You have an unlimited right to withdraw amounts from it.

However, if you receive a distribution from your deceased spouse's IRA, you can roll that distribution over into your own IRA within the 60-day time limit, as long as the distribution is not a required distribution, even if you are not the sole beneficiary of your deceased spouse's IRA. For more information, see *When Must You Withdraw Assets? (Required Minimum Distributions)* in Pub. 590-B for more information on required minimum distributions.

Inherited from Someone Other Than Spouse

If you inherit a traditional IRA from anyone other than your deceased spouse, you cannot treat the inherited IRA as

your own. This means that you cannot make any contributions to the IRA. It also means you cannot roll over any amounts into or out of the inherited IRA. However, you can make a trustee-to-trustee transfer as long as the IRA into which amounts are being moved is set up and maintained in the name of the deceased IRA owner for the benefit of you as beneficiary. See Pub. 590-B for more information.

Like the original owner, you generally will not owe tax on the assets in the IRA until you receive distributions from it. You must begin receiving distributions from the IRA under the rules for distributions that apply to beneficiaries.

More information. For more information about rollovers, required distributions, and inherited IRAs, see:

- *Rollovers*, later, under *Can You Move Retirement Plan Assets?*,

- *When Must You Withdraw Assets? (Required Minimum Distributions)* in Pub. 590-B, and

- The discussion of IRA Beneficiaries, under *When Must You Withdraw Assets? (Required Minimum Distributions)* in Pub. 590-B.

Can You Move Retirement Plan Assets?

You can transfer, tax free, assets (money or property) from other retirement programs (including traditional IRAs) to a traditional IRA. You can make the following kinds of transfers.

- Transfers from one trustee to another.

- Rollovers.

- Transfers incident to a divorce.

This chapter discusses all three kinds of transfers.

Transfers to Roth IRAs. Under certain conditions, you can move assets from a traditional IRA or from a designated Roth account to a Roth IRA. For more information about these transfers, see *Converting From Any Traditional IRA Into a Roth IRA*, later in this chapter, and *Can You Move Amounts Into a Roth IRA?* in chapter 2.

Transfers to Roth IRAs from other retirement plans. Under certain conditions, you can move assets from a qualified retirement plan to a Roth IRA. For more information, see *Can You Move Amounts Into a Roth IRA?* in chapter 2.

Trustee-to-Trustee Transfer

A transfer of funds in your traditional IRA from one trustee directly to another, either at your request or at the trustee's request, is not a rollover. This includes the situation where the current trustee issues a check to the new trustee but gives it to you to deposit. Because there is no distribution to you, the transfer is tax free. Because it is not a rollover, it is not affected by the 1-year waiting period required between rollovers. This waiting period is discussed later under *Rollover From One IRA Into Another*.

For information about direct transfers from retirement programs other than traditional IRAs, see *Direct rollover option*, later.

Rollovers

Generally, a rollover is a tax-free distribution to you of cash or other assets from one retirement plan that you contribute to another retirement plan. The contribution to the second retirement plan is called a "rollover contribution."

Note. An amount rolled over tax free from one retirement plan to another is generally includible in income when it is distributed from the second plan.

Kinds of rollovers to a traditional IRA. You can roll over amounts from the following plans into a traditional IRA:

* A traditional IRA,
* An employer's qualified retirement plan for its employees,
* A deferred compensation plan of a state or local government (section 457 plan), or
* A tax-sheltered annuity plan (section 403 plan).

Also, see Table 1-4, later.

Treatment of rollovers. You cannot deduct a rollover contribution, but you must report the rollover distribution on your tax return as discussed later under *Reporting rollovers from IRAs* and *Reporting rollovers from employer plans*.

Rollover notice. A written explanation of rollover treatment must be given to you by the plan (other than an IRA) making the distribution. See *Written explanation to recipients*, later, for more details.

Kinds of rollovers from a traditional IRA. You may be able to roll over, tax free, a distribution from your traditional IRA into a qualified plan. These plans include the Federal Thrift Savings Fund (for federal employees), deferred compensation plans of state or local governments (section 457 plans), and tax-sheltered annuity plans (section 403(b) plans). The part of the distribution that you can roll over is the part that would otherwise be taxable (includible in your income). Qualified plans may, but are not required to, accept such rollovers.

Tax treatment of a rollover from a traditional IRA to an eligible retirement plan other than an IRA. Ordinarily, when you have basis in your IRAs, any distribution is considered to include both nontaxable and taxable amounts. Without a special rule, the nontaxable portion of such a distribution could not be rolled over. However, a special rule treats a distribution you roll over into an eligible retirement plan as including only otherwise taxable amounts if the amount you either leave in your IRAs or do not roll over is at least equal to your basis. The effect of this special rule is to make the amount in your traditional IRAs that you can roll over to an eligible retirement plan as large as possible.

Eligible retirement plans. The following are considered eligible retirement plans.

* Individual retirement arrangements (IRAs).
* Qualified trusts.
* Qualified employee annuity plans under section 403(a).
* Deferred compensation plans of state and local governments (section 457 plans).
* Tax-sheltered annuities (section 403(b) annuities).

Time Limit for Making a Rollover Contribution

You generally must make the rollover contribution by the 60th day after the day you receive the distribution from your traditional IRA or your employer's plan.

Example. You received an eligible rollover distribution from your traditional IRA on June 30, 2016, that you intend to roll over to your 403(b) plan. To postpone including the distribution in your income, you must complete the rollover by August 29, 2016, the 60th day following June 30.

The IRS may waive the 60-day requirement where the failure to do so would be against equity or good conscience, such as in the event of a casualty, disaster, or other event beyond your reasonable control. For exceptions to the 60-day period, see *Ways to get a waiver of the 60-day rollover requirement*, later.

Rollovers completed after the 60-day period. In the absence of a waiver, amounts not rolled over within the 60-day period do not qualify for tax-free rollover treatment. You must treat them as a taxable distribution from either your IRA or your employer's plan. These amounts are taxable in the year distributed, even if the 60-day period expires in the next year. You may also have to pay a 10% additional tax on early distributions as discussed under *Early Distributions* in Pub. 590-B.

Unless there is a waiver or an extension of the 60-day rollover period, any contribution you make to your IRA more than 60 days after the distribution is a regular contribution, not a rollover contribution.

Example. You received a distribution in late December 2016 from a traditional IRA that you do not roll over

Chapter 1   **Traditional IRAs**   Page 21

If you don't do anything about your IRA, you are basically telling the IRS just how much you love them. Your great love gift goes to them first, after all. They benefit the most. Do you love the IRS more than your spouse and your kids? The IRS thinks so.

Now, back to John. When I met John he was an 82-year-old widower with four grown children, seven grandchildren, and approximately $350,000 in that IRA of his. There had been more in there at one point, but his wife had taken a turn for the worse near the end, and so he did what any good husband would do: he broke into the Never Bucket and took out everything she needed.

Now that he was alone, however, he really didn't need the money. He lived frugally, and he only took out $30,000 a year from the IRA because that was the mandatory minimum. He had no choice in the matter. He'd started putting some of the money aside in a savings account because he couldn't think what else to do with it.

He probably would have continued doing just that, but he'd heard a bit about me from a friend of his, he was feeling anxious about how his finances looked, and so he came into my office. we sat down together and went through the bucket story together, and of course, he didn't want any money to go to the IRS. So, I asked him the truth: if that was the case then why was the IRS his first beneficiary. He couldn't believe it. He looked over his paperwork. No, he told me, the IRS wasn't on there. It was just his four kids.

I had to break it to him. I said, "John, the fact is, the IRS gets the first cut off of your IRA. That's how they've set it up. It's why they call themselves 'the IRS.' Look at it another way, and it spells out 'THEIRS.' Right now, with your IRA, you're looking at gifting about $100,000 to the government through taxes. When you die and leave that IRA to your kids, they're going to have to pay that. You said you want to split that money four ways between your kids, well, after they take out that $100,000, they're only going to get about $62,500 each. That's about $25,000 less than you expected them to get."

He tried to correct me at that point. He told me one of his friends had inherited a whole IRA from her spouse without losing a cent. He, like a lot of people, thought he had the financial side of things mostly figured out at his point in life.

So I showed him what I'm going to show you now. If you look at Form 590, you'll see that a spouse can inherit an IRA without paying tax, but only a spouse. John's kids weren't going to get away from the IRS with all of that IRA money. That's what the second highlighted portion of the text tells you. If you inherit IRA from anyone other than your spouse, you cannot make it your own. You have to convert it into an inherited IRA and that means you're going to start paying taxes.

It's hard to disappoint a nice 82-year-old man, but I felt I had to do it. I let him take in the truth for a few moments before I gave him the good news.

"Look, John, I know that's hard to take," I told him, "but the upside is that we still have an opportunity to correct that."

He brightened up as soon as I explained how it worked. By now, you know the trick by heart, I'm sure. We used the **5% Solution** to take just a little bit out of his IRA, from his Never Bucket, and we put that directly into the tax-free Harvest Bucket via a life insurance policy. And with that, he was suddenly able to get up to $500,000 of tax-free money.

Pennsylvania State Asset Protection Statues

The Richardson Group
Wealth Protection

Life Insurance

42 PA Cons Stat § 8124(C)(4)

(4) Any amount of proceeds retained by the insurer at maturity or otherwise under the terms of an annuity or policy of life insurance if the policy or a supplemental agreement provides that such proceeds and the income therefrom shall not be assignable.

42 PA Cons Stat § 8124(C)(6)

(6) The net amount payable under any annuity contract or policy of life insurance made for the benefit of or assigned to the spouse, children or dependent relative of the insured, whether or not the right to change the named beneficiary is reserved by or permitted to the insured. The preceding sentence shall not be applicable to the extent the judgment debtor is such spouse, child or other relative.

42 PA Cons Stat § 8124(5)

(5) Any policy of group insurance or the proceeds thereof.

Annuity

42 PA Cons Stat § 8124(C)

(c) Insurance proceeds. --The following property or other rights of the judgment debtor shall be exempt from attachment or execution on a judgment:

(1) Certain amounts paid, provided or rendered by a fraternal benefit society as provided by 40 Pa.C.S. § 6531 (relating to benefits not attachable).

(2) Claims and compensation payments under the act of June 2, 1915 (P.L.736, No.338), known as "The Pennsylvania Workmen's Compensation Law," except as otherwise provided in the act.

(3) Any policy or contract of insurance or annuity issued to a solvent insured who is the beneficiary thereof, except any part thereof exceeding an income or return of $100 per month.

(4) Any amount of proceeds retained by the insurer at maturity or otherwise under the terms of an annuity or policy of life insurance if the policy or a supplemental agreement provides that such proceeds and the income therefrom shall not be assignable.

(5) Any policy of group insurance or the proceeds thereof.

(6) The net amount payable under any annuity contract or policy of life insurance made for the benefit of or assigned to the spouse, children or dependent relative of the insured, whether or not the right to change the named beneficiary is reserved by or permitted to the insured. The preceding sentence shall not be applicable to the extent the judgment debtor is such spouse, child or other relative.

(7) The net amount payable under any accident or disability insurance.

The Richardson Group | 405 Murry Hill Dr., Lancaster, PA 17601
(717) 394-0840 | www.financialadvisorlancaster.com

(8) Certain amounts paid, provided or rendered by a fraternal benefit society as provided by section 305 of the act of July 29, 1977 (P.L.105, No.38), known as the "Fraternal Benefit Society Code."

(9) Certain amounts paid, provided or rendered under the provisions of section 106(f) of the act of July 19, 1974 (P.L.489, No.176), known as the "Pennsylvania No-fault Motor Vehicle Insurance Act."

(10) Certain amounts paid, provided or rendered under the provisions of section 703 of the act of December 5, 1936 (2nd Sp.Sess., 1937 P.L.2897, No.1), known as the "Unemployment Compensation Law."

(Apr. 28, 1978, P.L.202, No.53, eff. 60 days; Oct. 5, 1980, P.L.693, No.142, eff. 60 days; Dec. 20, 1982, P.L.1409, No.326, eff. 60 days; Oct. 12, 1990, P.L.531, No.128, eff. 60 days; Feb. 18, 1998, P.L.170, No.26, eff. imd.; Dec. 20, 2000, P.L.742, No.105, eff. 60 days)

IRA

42 PA Cons Stat § 8124(b)(i)(ix)

(ix) Any retirement or annuity fund provided for under section 401(a), 403(a) and (b), 408, 408A, 409 or 530 of the Internal Revenue Code of 1986 (Public Law 99-514, 26 U.S.C. § 401(a), 403(a) and (b), 408, 408A, 409 or 530), the appreciation thereon, the income therefrom, the benefits or annuity payable thereunder and transfers and rollovers between such funds. This subparagraph shall not apply to:

(A) Amounts contributed by the debtor to the retirement or annuity fund within one year before the debtor filed for bankruptcy. This shall not include amounts directly rolled over from other funds which are exempt from attachment under this subparagraph.

(B) Amounts contributed by the debtor to the retirement or annuity fund in excess of $15,000 within a one-year period. This shall not include amounts directly rolled over from other funds which are exempt from attachment under this subparagraph.

(C) Amounts deemed to be fraudulent conveyances.

(2) The exemptions provided by paragraph (1)(i) through (vi) shall be subject to any inconsistent provision of the act of July 8, 1978 (P.L.752, No.140), known as the "Public Employee Pension Forfeiture Act."

When I told him the amount, he smiled at me. He told me that before his wife got sick, $500,000 was what he had had in his IRA, and that was the amount he and his wife had always hoped to reach to pass down to their kids. The fact he could do that now, well, you can imagine how happy he was to get that money back to provide for his kids. In a way, he was able to honor his wife by doing that. It meant a lot more than just money to him.

Now, his family will get what is left in the IRA after taxes plus all that tax-free money. They're going to be able to benefit in a more substantial way than they would have if they just got the IRA. All that, and it didn't change the amount he was drawing on his IRA. It didn't change the fact that he'd have money if he needed it to pay for to treat a terminal illness, or to get assisted care in the home, or to move to an assisted living facility or a nursing home. He had the money set aside for him, for taxes, and for his kids. He was set.

But John, being a smart man, wanted to know if there was anything else I could do for him, which of course there was. I asked him if he was happy with his IRA. Well, before he walked in the door, he probably would have answered unequivocally "yes," but now he told me he wasn't so sure.

"What are you offering instead?"

"Well, John, how do you feel about fees?"

He hated them, of course, but he told me that was the price of doing business. I told him it wasn't. I told him that an indexed annuity would keep his money safe in a way his IRA variable annuity couldn't, so he wouldn't have to worry about losses or fees of any kind, and he could still draw out the same amount.

"Sounds great," he said, "but I don't want to pay all that tax."

Now it was my turn to smile, because I got to give John a great bit of news on that account. I showed him Form 590 again, and I pointed to that last page where it said Trustee-to-Trustee Transfer. What that means is, I could move his money from an IRA to an indexed annuity and there was no tax for him to pay. It goes from the old trustee to the new trustee, and it wouldn't show up on his tax return.

I told him to think about an IRA as a cup and in that cup you can put milk or you can put orange juice or you could put coffee. Let's say that where you are at now is coffee so we're going to pour the coffee out and we're going to pour milk in. We don't change the characteristic of the investment, we just change the type of investment it did. If you're in a mutual fund or a veritable annuity IRA and you're concerned you're going to lose money, we can exchange that IRA tax-free and put you into an indexed annuity where you don't have any fees. You don't have any losses to worry about, and your money is safe. You're just exchanging the IRA in your cup for the same amount of indexed annuity, which is more appropriate to you.

"We're not changing the characteristic of the tax," I told him, "All we did was make it safe. We made it safe, and now you can feel even more secure when we start taking 5% out to fund your life insurance."

Well, now I had truly made John's day. Since he was in such a great mood, I asked him to write a letter to his kids sharing the good news, and I asked if I could share it here. He agreed.

Dear Kids,

I am writing to you today to come clean about some serious worries I had about the state of my finances. I know you are all fully grown and have families of your own by now, and you don't need my money, but it's important to me that I leave you enough to help take care of all of you, at least a little bit. You mother and I managed to scrimp and save $500,000 over our working lifetimes. Unfortunately, when she got sick, some of that money had to be used for her care, and as of yesterday, I had only $350,000 left in my IRA.

Well, that number has changed today. After talking to my financial planner, I discovered that 100% of that money is subject to income taxes. I had, maybe foolishly, assumed it would pass directly to you all, just as I'd seen friends' IRAs pass to others. It turns out, that's only for spouses. For all of you, you would have owed the IRS an estimated $100,000 in income tax on my IRA prior to you using those funds for yourself.

I just couldn't live with that, seeing that much money disappear that your mother and I had worked so hard to give to you.

Thankfully, I don't have to live with it. Thanks to my new financial planner, Philip, I've been able to transfer my IRA to an indexed annuity, where I won't have any more fees and I won't be exposed to risks that might lose me more of your money. At the same time, I'm taking a small portion out of that account and buying life insurance. This life insurance policy will provide you with $500,000 of tax-free, probate-free cash. All of it will go to the four of you, split evenly. And you get to keep the annuity money after taxes.

It's so much more than I thought I'd ever be able to leave you. I feel really blessed right now.

To break down the numbers a little for you, the life insurance policy that I am talking about will increase your after tax inheritance from $250,000 with the IRA to $500,000. An increase of $250,000, or 100%.

In addition to that, you get to keep whatever remains of the IRA annuity money. I say "whatever is left" because I am allowed to use this money ($200,000 for long term care coverage or $250,000 for terminal illness coverage) if needed. That means you guys will never have to worry about breaking the bank to take care of your old man. If needed, I've been told I also have access to 90% of the cash that builds up in the plan. So, I'm set, and even if I use up all that money, you'll still have the life insurance coming your way.

So, that's it, kids. I hope that's all clear for you. Honestly, I thought I had this financial stuff down until I sat down with Philip. Now I know I have my money invested right for you guys and for me.

Oh, here's an interesting tidbit for you. I found out that Malcolm Forbes had $55,000,000 of life insurance in force when he died. How about that? Not a bad example to follow, I must say.

All of My Love,
Dad

I love this story, and that's why I wanted to dedicate the chapter entirely to John. John managed, in one visit, to get rid of fees on his account, add money to his inheritors, and disinherit the IRS. Not a bad day for John, right?

And, in essence, after all that, all we did was follow that farmer's advice from the beginning of the book. We just used the **5% Solution** to take out the seed so we wouldn't have to pay on the harvest.

That's all it took, and now John is set, literally for life. Even if he never makes a new penny in his new annuity, all he's losing is 5% of his Never Bucket money, and look at all he's gaining. His money will at least last 20 years, which would be a pretty good run for John.

And, it's extremely unlikely that he won't make any money. If he doesn't make money here, no one is making money in the market. No one would be in a better position. That's just how an indexed annuity works.

Essentially, it will cover you for your whole life. And if John uses it all up, fine, he's still got $500,000 set aside for his kids.

Chapter 5

Taking Care of Your End of Life Care

There's an uncomfortable reality that we all have to face at some point, at least if we want to act financially responsible. No, I'm not talking about death and taxes now, I'm talking about what happens before that. The reality is that during your lifetime, either you, your spouse, or both of you is most likely going to need assistance meeting your daily needs, whether it's in the home or an assisted living facility, or eventually in a nursing home.

When I tell people this, and I ask them what the likelihood is that they're going to need care they always estimate low. That makes sense. After all, when I ask them this, they're healthy, they're in good shape, they feel good. They just can't ever envision themselves being infirm. Even if they could imagine it, nobody's ever going to admit that they're going to be infirm when they're meeting with me in my office. It's an embarrassing thing to admit. People feel ashamed that it could happen to them. So, they brush it off and tell me, essentially, that it might happen to other people, but it's not going to happen to them, so why worry?

This is, in its own way, the same deflection the minister took when it came to finding a way to take care of his wife. The problem just wasn't worth thinking deeply about to him, and many of my clients instinctively feel the same way about long-term care.

It's my job, then, to try to illustrate that the probability they will need long-term care is far higher than they think. As you can already tell from this book, I like to tell stories. So, I tell my clients another little story, this one is called "the airplane story," and it's about taking a journey. Just like your journey through your life from now to the end, and in between now and the end, certain things can happen. We don't know what will happen, but anything could. Just like on an airplane.

But, of course, when we get on an airplane, we know how unlikely it is anything will go wrong. Or, we think we know that. Let's say you're taking this journey somewhere. Pick any place you like. Your dream location that you've been waiting to visit for your whole life. Let's say it's Paris.

So, you've packed your bags. You've fought your way through the traffic to the airport. And as you park and walk through the airport doors, you're finally starting to get really excited. Paris never felt closer. You feel like you're almost there. Of course, you still have to do all those crazy little things to get through the airport. You stand in line and check your bags, you head to security and take off your shoes, take off your belt. You stand in line again, you deal with the impatient people yelling around you. You show your identification whenever requested.

Eventually, you make it through security, and you're sitting around waiting for the plane. They call your flight, and after standing in another line, looking at your ticket, you notice that you're in the last group to get called on. Everybody else boarded in front of you. You are barely able to find the place for your carry-on luggage when you get on the plane. You have to climb over two individuals to get to your seat.

Finally, you're in your seat and you can relax a little bit. After all, the worst is over. Paris is just a few short hours away. You've gone through all the tough stuff already.

As you're getting ready to take off, the pilot comes on over the intercom. He sounds nice and relaxed. He's bright and friendly. He tells a couple jokes and apologizes for all the delays you and the other passengers had to deal with. Then, he gives you the overview of the trip.

"Well, folks, we're looking at an 8-hour flight together. We're going to be traveling at 600 miles an hour. We're going to be at 37,000 feet. We have clear skies over the Atlantic, and things are looking good."

It's all the standard stuff, and you're about to tune him out when your ear picks up a change in his voice. The pilot clears his throat and says, "Oh yeah, and one more thing I think I should make you aware of. We really only have about a 50% chance of arriving safely at our destination today. Have a great flight, folks!"

When you hear that and the whole plane hears that, people start running for the exits. Forget Paris. Nobody is going to fly on an airplane that admits they only have 50-50 shot of arriving safely at their destination. All the sudden, you're crawling over people, leaving your luggage behind, you're fleeing as fast as you can because those odds are terrible, and you're not going to risk them, not even to get to your dream location.

Well, what if I told you those are about the odds that you or your spouse will end up needing long-term care? With those odds, one of you (and there's a decent chance both of you) is going to need assistance prior to the end of your life, whether it's in your home, or in an assisted living facility, or in a nursing home.

Now that we understand that, let's think about how we're going to resolve this issue. What are we going to do if we need care? Once I have people on the same page with me, most of them will give me their honest answer. In different words, of course, they will tell me that they have a Never Bucket, and that's the money they'll use when the time comes.

I think that's a great plan. As you know, I'm a big fan of the Never Bucket. However, using that money may not be as straightforward as people believe. After all, we know by now, there are often taxes connected to that Never Bucket that will decrease the available amount significantly. Even if that isn't necessarily a concern, that Never Bucket may not have enough money in it to take care of you and your spouse. But before we get into that. Let's talk a little bit about what the types of care might look like up ahead for your or your spouse.

First of all, people don't normally jump from healthy living into a nursing home. Instead, it's usually a gradual process that can take years (and as we'll see, a lot of money). The three stages are: in-home care, assisted living, and then the nursing home. Not everyone goes through all three stages, but they do usually chart a gradual decline in health.

So, let's begin with in-home care. That becomes a necessary option when you have issues where you need someone to come by during certain times during the day or week and care for you in the home. This becomes necessary when you or your spouse struggle to complete some of the six activities of daily living.

The six activities are:

1. Feeding yourself

2. Bathing yourself

3. Dressing yourself

4. Toileting yourself (including getting to, on and off the toilet)

5. Transferring yourself (getting in and out of bed, getting from one room to another)

6. Maintaining continence

If you struggle with any of those, then you qualify or need in-home assistance.

Essentially, if you reach a point where you find you have trouble cooking for yourself, or you can't get around really well because you have a bad leg or a bad hip, that's when you need to investigate some care in your home. At this point, you can still stay in your own home and live on your own (or with your spouse), but you will need someone to stop by at set times to help you with certain tasks.

Assisted living comes into play when you have to have more regular assistance. Maybe it's a memory issue, where you need someone to make sure you take your medication on time. Maybe it's a feeding issue where you don't just have trouble cooking but now you have have trouble feeding yourself or swallowing. You're not so bad that you need to go to a nursing home, because you can get around, you can do things for yourself, but your health is degrading enough that you need a more regular presence for assistance.

With assisted living, you're in an apartment somewhere, and you have more people keeping an eye on you on a regular basis. You're no longer able to stay in your home, but you're still relatively autonomous and comfortable. You have nursing staff there, as well as non-nursing staff. They're making sure that all of your needs of living are met. You need some assistance with making sure you're getting fed. Maybe they're providing meal service, or they're having somebody come in to feed you. They're making sure that your hygiene is taken care of. They're doing those kind of issues. You get care in your apartment, and otherwise you're left to yourself.

Of course, eventually, gradually, your health will continue to degrade to the point you need constant care. Maybe your memory issue expands into a full diagnosis of Alzheimer's, and you have to be watched 24/7. Or perhaps your health simply deteriorates to the point you can't get around anymore. A lot of times, people say they fell and broke their hip, but the reality is they break their hip, then they fall down because their bones are brittle. That is an unfortunately common set of events that essentially put you on you back for a long while. And once you're on your back for too long, then your muscles don't work anymore, and you never really get out of bed. It's events like that that lead to the last stage, to the nursing home.

Once you're in a nursing home, you can be there for any amount of time. For some people, it's a short stay, but for others, life in the nursing home can go on for years. In our case, Helen was there eight and a half years before she passed.

Financially, each of these three stages is quite expensive. Home care is an hourly rate, so you're paying something around $50 an hour for non-nursing care to come to your house. If you need assistance ten hours a week, you're looking at $2,000 a month.

Then, assisted living tends to be between $3,500 and $5,000 a month. That's essentially half of the cost of a nursing home, which is usually about $10,000 a month. So, at each stage, the cost doubles. Keep in mind, Medicaid will only help you with the nursing home. The two stages before that will be dependent upon your finances.

That's the general path from health to the nursing home. It's not a very pretty or elegant picture I've painted, I know, but it's important for you to be aware of what end of life care looks like. Again, this affects almost 50% of people. Those are pretty daunting odds, so you should be prepared on a financial level to take care of yourself and/or your spouse.

If I told you that there was a 50% chance that your bank would close next year, you'd take the money out and put it elsewhere, right? You'd do what you had to to protect your money for yourself and your family. And if I said there was a 50% chance your house would burn down, you'd move, no matter how much you loved the house. Well, end of life care is your 50% chance. What are you going to do to protect yourself?

A good place to start is where we can just take a little bit of that seed from your Never Bucket, pay the tax on it, and put that into a tax-free Harvest Bucket that then allows you to draw money in the event you need care in your home or in a facility. Once you do that, you have another checkbook that you can draw from. By doing the things outlined in this book, you've already positioned yourself to protect the money you have, but that's not the only resource that's available to you.

Even if you're in a nursing home or in a assisted living care, you still have some opportunities to protect your money.

That's right, even in a nursing home, there are ways to protect your assets. This is what Cathy and I wish we'd known about when we were taking care of Helen for all those years. As I explained in the introduction, we took care of Helen for eight years as her health declined. During all that time, we took the burden on ourselves. We paid for in-home care when we needed it, but mostly we took care of her ourselves. We transformed our lives, and we received nothing for it. Not that we were looking for anything, but some income from Helen to help ease the costs would have done a great deal for us and our young family.

Helen's health problems caught us unawares, just as they often do for people. She had always been strong and independent, until she suddenly wasn't anymore. Watching her health decline, especially her mental health, was hard. She's an excellent example of a person you'd never have assumed would need long-term care. And yet, she was in that 50% in the end.

Unfortunately, as time went on, she continued to become an increasing burden for us, and it was hard on her as well. I often wish we'd known about the strategies I'm about to outline for you. For Helen's sake, I try to spread the word as much as possible now, so that others can have a little less to struggle with in those final years with their loved ones.

So, without any more introduction, let's get to those strategies that could have helped my family, and which can still help yours.

First, during those years of in-home care, there is a benefit that is available called "aid attendance." If you were a veteran during a declared state of war, as Helen was, and you served even just one day during that time period and 90 days on reserve thereafter, you are entitled to a fully paid up long-term care policy that pays about $2,600 a month for home care or assisted living. It also pays in a nursing home. For those of you doing the math, that would be enough to cover your entire in-home care costs. It would also be most of what's required for your assisted living costs.

However, like many benefits with the government, it isn't always the easiest to acquire. You can, by all means, go and apply for this benefit on your own. Your local VA will be very nice, and they'll fill out all the papers for you, but I guarantee they'll come back and stamped "over-resourced."

That means, according to the VA, you have too much money. When you go back in and ask your friendly representative at the VA, "What can I do to fix it?" They will kindly respond, "I have no idea because we work with the VA, and the VA doesn't tell us one way or another."

To get this benefit, you need someone like me who can show you how. Even if you're over-resourced today, we can do some rearrangements with your assets and use different kinds of annuities. You may be under-resourced tomorrow.

By all means, go into your VA and apply for yourself today. There currently is no look-back on veterans' benefits, so if you want to apply on your own and try to save yourself some money, go right ahead. But when it comes back rejected, just be sure to come to my office so we can fill that application out the right way and get you the benefits you deserve.

There's no worry about delays. We can reapply the next day after we rearrange your finances, and then you'll get back a form that says, "You've been approved." Then, you'll have the money available to pay for a lot of the care you need, either in your home or in a facility.

By the way, this isn't just a benefit for the spouse who served. If your spouse served but you did not, you're entitled to one half of the benefit. That's a great benefit in recognition of that fact that one spouse had to hold down the home fires while the other was off serving their country.

It's a great benefit, and if you are a veteran, or the spouse of a veteran, I encourage you to come in so I can provide some more information and we can see if you qualify. However, there is one catch. Unlike most of the strategies in this book, there's not much you can do for this one until the moment comes when you need care. Until you need care either in the home or a facility, there are no forms to fill out or finances to rearrange. We can't do anything until that happens.

Of course, whether you're a veteran or not, that $2,600 won't cover your nursing home bills. The story everyone hears is that nursing homes take all your money before they'll help you. That's often the case, but don't worry, I have a strategy to help you with that as well.

Once you're in a situation where you or your spouse needs to enter a nursing home, the words you're going to hear all the time are "spend down." Basically, they're going to require you to spend down your assets to a predetermined amount. When you're married, that's generally $120,000. If you're not married, that's all the way down to $2,000. Say goodbye to that money you saved to give to your family. Say goodbye to all your assets. The nursing home wants it all.

I know you're concerned about how you're going to protect yourself from this. Most people think they can't protect themselves. They resign themselves to this possibility, and hope they aren't in the 50% who need it (or whatever percent they assume is correct).

Thankfully, you don't just have to hope and then become re-signed. I can assist you to protect, if you're married, 100% of your assets from spend down on a nursing home. Even if you aren't married, I can protect 50% of your assets. That's a lot better than spending down to $2,000, isn't it?

Let me tell you about one client I had. He had $1,500,000 saved up for him and his wife. When it came time for him to go to the nursing home, the nursing home was very happy to take him as a resident because of his asset size. They assumed they'd be getting all but a small chunk of that, so you can imagine how they rolled out the red carpet for him.

Unfortunately for them, they had to re-cork all that champagne they had opened because within a month, we had changed the assets around to the spouse. And just like with the VA, there's no look back to allow them to change their decision after it's been made. We were able to transfer the money through an annuity right away while also making my client eligible for Medicaid. We did this through what's called a Medicaid Compliant Annuity, which allowed him to transfer all of his wealth to her, and at the same time making all of it exempt from the nursing home. It allowed him to be on Medicaid, while she got to keep $1,500,000.

For those of you who are widows and widowers, you still don't have to resign yourself to losing everything by "spending down." You can still protect a lot of your money, it just requires us to do what's called half a loaf planning. The married couple gets the whole loaf, the single spouse that's left is going to get the half a loaf, which means, essentially, we're saving half of the money that would have gone to the nursing home. I'm able to save that for your family, so you don't have to worry about leaving them with nothing.

These strategies really work, and they can make all the difference in the last few years of your life. Often, the system can feel arbitrary and unfair if you aren't being guided through it. Reasonable assumptions you might make about how you are protected and how safe your money is can prove completely wrong when it's too late to do anything.

Take, for example, the story of the two veterans: William and Bob. Both William and Bob served their country. They both acquitted themselves with honor and returned home to live their lives. One of them, William, was a saver. And William saved up his money until he had quite a bit tucked away. Like most people, he scrimped and saved. When he reached retirement age, he thought he was set. But then, he got sick. It turned out, he had developed Alzheimer's. When he needed care, because he had saved up his money, he had to use all of that money to take care of himself.

Now Bob, he was never a saver. He didn't have any money. He enjoyed himself and spent almost every penny by the time he reached retirement. Then, Bob had a heart attack. Well, the government saw Bob had no money, so the government paid all of his bills. Bob walked out the hospital no worse off than he was the day before (at least not financially), while William lost everything and saved for no reason.

Why did this happen? The reason is that Medicare will pay for you if you have a heart attack, but it won't cover long-term care. The government doesn't care how hard you worked or how much you saved, a decision has been made to cover some medical issues but not to cover long-term care, and as far as the government is concerned, you're just out of luck if you need care and you wanted to protect your savings.

So, let me ask you something: is that fair? If you can't get around your house, or you have Alzheimer's, the government doesn't want to pay for that. If they can cut you open and fix you up quickly, they'll fork out the money for you, but they aren't interested in helping you with chronic problems, no matter how good a citizen you've been. Does it seem fair to you that the government picks winners and losers when it comes to medical diagnoses?

Because to me it doesn't. It seems pretty arbitrary, and it seems to punish most the people who did everything right.

It's part of my job to make the system a little fairer. Whether you had a heart attack or have Alzheimer's, it shouldn't be your responsibility to pay that bill, and in fact, you don't have to pay it. We can use these rules and make some changes to even out the field for you and provide some protection that you would otherwise not have.

I can switch things around, so that you can qualify for care and you don't have to use your own money in the event you have Alzheimer's, and didn't have a heart attack. Essentially, I make sure that both William and Bob end up with what they started out with when they got sick. To me, if William worked so hard to save, William deserves to have that money. It's just that simple.

I know this particular issue can sometimes feel a little complicated, so here's one more story to spell it out a little clearer for you. This one involves a couple named George and Rebecca.

George and Rebecca had been together for more than forty years when George's Parkinson's progressed to the point he needed to be in a nursing home. For Rebecca, that was a double blow. Not only was her husband being taken away from her, but she was worried she'd lose everything now that he was going.

Together, George and Rebecca had accumulated about $200,000 in savings, plus a house, a car, and their other possessions. When she came in to see me, she was worried all of that she'd lose all of that. She had been on the phone with her kids, trying to find out which one she would have to move in with.

I calmed her down and let her know that even in the worst "spend down" situation, she would still be able to keep $120,000, as well as the house, the car, and all their possessions.

She was obviously relieved and ready to consider that good enough, but I stopped her before she could get out the door. When I told her she didn't have to lose anything, well, you can imagine how that piqued her interest.

Right there and then, I laid out for her the strategy for transferring all of her and George's savings that were above the $120,000 limit into a Medicaid Compliant Annuity. Once she did that, all of her money was safe, and George was able to go to the nursing home without any guilty feelings of depriving his wife of their hard earned money.

It's just that simple really. The reason you never hear about this option is that people like Rebecca go to the nursing home first to find out about what their options look like, and the nursing home has no incentive to show them the correct way to save their assets. What they're going to do is make you spend all of your money so that they can benefit before they move you over to Medicaid. What we do is make you Medicaid eligible in advance, essentially right after your admission to a nursing home. For obvious reasons, nursing homes aren't eager to mention that possibility to anyone.

It isn't just nursing homes, though. Surprisingly, many experts in the field don't know how this works. I once hired the lady who ran the Medicaid office of our county. She was the administrator for 16 years there and was making sure that the county and state got every penny that they were entitled to from your assets.

After leaving there, she went and worked for an elder law attorney in the county for nine years on a full-time basis. So, when she came and worked for me, you'd assume she knew all there was to know about how this process worked. Yet, when I sat down and told her about it, she couldn't believe it.

I told her, "Here's how we help people. When we have a married couple, we can use a certain kind of annuity that will protect 100% of their assets from spend down at the nursing home."

When I was finished explaining it to her, she said, "You know, you're not allowed to do that."

"You have to be kidding me," I said. "What do you mean 'you're not allowed to do that?'"

"You have to spend down, and that's all we were doing at the law firm was helping people to spend down their assets."

So, all the law firm was doing was helping people put a new roof on their house or buy a new car or do those kind of things, but they didn't have any strategy for protecting your money. She didn't even know it was possible. After all those years working in the field, it was a complete revelation for her.

When I told this new employee of mine all about these strategies, she couldn't believe it. When I related the stories I told you above, she still struggled to believe it. It took me about two weeks of research and articles to convince her that you could actually use these kinds of strategies. She was amazed that this was available.

It's not a surprise that non financial professionals are not necessarily in the know on this because these are financial strategies. Just as I don't know most attorney strategies, I couldn't expect her to know any financial strategies walking in the door. But I know she's glad I showed her how it works, because it made her more aware of how to help people.

This may seem like a meaningless point, but it's important because I've known many clients who think they can get everything done through just one person. I'll talk about this more in the next chapter, but keep in mind for now, when you need to go to an attorney, you should look for an elder law attorney that has a basic understanding of the financial strategies you want to employ. They don't have to take care of those strategies for you (that's what I'm here for), but make sure you're getting good advice from someone who understands what you need not just legally but financially going forward.

When you're dealing with advisors, you want to make sure that they understand Medicaid, how to get it, and how to help you apply for it. Because that's really the only way you can save wealth in a nursing home.

You need these strategies to help you level the playing field. Make sure everyone you work with is on board with that.

This is crucial because if you don't have smart advisors who know what they're doing, there's a lot of potential risk for you. There are plenty of cases where the transfers were not done properly, and the government came after people's family to get the money back. There are even laws on the books in some states called filial laws, which state the government can go after the child to pay for the parents' care in a nursing home.

I'm sure this is the exact opposite of what you want for your kids. In fact, it's the nightmare scenario. As you can see, there are some excellent reasons to go to someone who knows exactly how to shift your money into the right accounts to protect that money and protect your family.

Chapter 6

Estate Planning

We've reached the final chapter, and here, I'd like to take a little time to draw the many strands of this book together and talk in a general sense about your estate.

When we talk about an estate, we're talking about your entire financial picture, not just as many people assume, an investment plan. Estate planning encompasses retirement planning, investment planning, and risk planning. It's a comprehensive review of how your money will take care of you now and move to your beneficiaries later. In other words, it's the main theme of this book.

We've talked a lot about the best strategies to maximize the assets in your estate in this book. We've covered how you should be investing your money now that you are retired, how you should limit your risk, and how you should prepare your finances for health issues ahead. At the same time, we've been leading up to one important question: what's going to happen to your assets at your death? Who are you transferring your money to, and how are you going to do it?

I think by now you're sold on the idea of getting as much out of your harvest as possible and giving as little to the taxman as you legally can. So, how do we do that when transferring your estate? How do we transfer your money in the most tax efficient manner possible?

It's great to grow your money, it's great to have a plan for retirement to do this or to do that, but ultimately, what it comes down to is, how is your wealth going to leave your care and move onto someone else's care?

You know all this, of course. If you weren't worrying about this, you wouldn't have read this book. You know that if done improperly, the loss to your heirs can be really, really economically devastating. Think of some of the numbers we've highlighted in this book. Hundreds of thousands of dollars could have been lost in some cases. In one, over a million dollars could have been lost. It wasn't, because the people I highlighted in this book listened to and followed the strategies I recommended. I hope you'll do the same.

What we want to do now is make sure that your estate plan is one that you understand completely. What I mean is, do you know all of the ways your funds are going to be transferred? If not, you need someone to help explain this to you. That way, if you don't like something, we have an opportunity to fix things before it's too late.

If you're looking for reasons why you should take care of this now and not put it off, I have plenty of examples for you of people that did not plan their estates properly. Do you recognize any of these names?

Robin Williams, Michael Jackson, Kurt Cobain.

That is just the tip of the iceberg in terms of well-known celebrities who died without having their estates in order. And what did these famous people do wrong? First, they didn't have a will. That's step number one for anyone who wants to pass anything along to their heirs. Do you have a will? If you don't, you need to address that right away. I'm telling you that even though I don't do wills. I can, however, make sure you speak to the right people to help you write one. If you don't have a will now, I'll get you to an attorney that can get it done for you.

So, that's the first thing you need to do that these celebrities didn't do. Second, do you have a power of attorney? That's another legal document you need to have. Just having the document isn't enough either. You need to make sure your power of attorney allows for unlimited gifting between spouses. That's crucial, and another issue that heirs of those who don't plan end up having to deal with.

Finally, do you have a healthcare proxy? Have you predetermined the kind of medical care you'd like to receive in the event you're not able to make those decisions for yourself?

Those are three basic estate planning documents you ought to have settled not tomorrow, not today, but yesterday. Even if you have all that done, there's still a lot we need to work through with your estate. We need to look at how are your assets titled. Who is the owner or joint owner of your property? How is that going to pass in your death? How are your investments titled? Is it just you, are you going to leave them through your will to a beneficiary? If you do, that means they go through probate. What are the beneficiary designations? And who are the beneficiaries?

We have to review all of these strategies (and more) to make sure your money is going where you want it to and everything is in line with your wishes. To do that properly is a process, which includes going through your bank accounts, your investments, your annuities, your home, your cars, any collectibles. Everything you have has to be detailed in some fashion.

As you can see, it's not necessarily the fastest or most convenient process, that's why the above celebrities didn't do it. It's also why you can hire me to simplify the process for you. If you don't resolve these issues, your estate could end up just like one of those celebrities' estates: tied up in court for years. And keep in mind, the longer an estate is tied up, the more the legal fees rise and eat up the value of that estate. These things can take years, if not decades, to finally close out. Think of the suffering those families are going through because of the mistakes that those celebrities made.

There's are a couple reasons there's such a blind spot when it comes to estates, even those of the rich and famous. First, once again, people don't want to be brave and wise enough to face their mortality. Second, just like everything else in this book, people just don't hear about all the strategies they need to protect their assets. You're not going get this advice from Edward Jones because the advisers there can't give it to you. They're not allowed to because, as we discussed earlier in the book, they're not independent. Their bosses tell them what to do.

You can (and should) go to an attorney, and while they will help you with those legal documents, they won't be able to advise you on the financial side of things, which, as we discussed in the last chapter, can lead to some major oversights. Lawyers aren't trained to understand annuities. They can get your will in order, but for your investments, you need someone like me.

What you really need is a lawyer and a financial adviser who can work together. Thankfully, that's possible if you come to me. I have a relationship with an attorney down the street who oversees Medicaid planning, wills, and power of attorney. Everyone who becomes a Medicaid Case Client gets to see a lawyer for free; I pay the fee. That's right, I cover it. All you have to do is go down the street and get your documents in order. By the time you get there, I've already told him in advance what your situation is and what you need.

And with that point made, we've arrived at the final pages of our final chapter. I really hope you take advantage of the information that I've provided you today in this book. After all, information is great, but action is better.

In order to encourage you to take that first major step towards improving the outlook of your estate, I'm offering to drop my entire advisor fee. That means you'll save **$595** and get a free consultation where we can get together and review your situation in detail to see what I can do to help you.

Because you took the opportunity to read this book and spent some time evaluating on your own, even before you decided to work with me, I know you're going to be the type of person I can help. So, I'll waive my fee. All you have to do is show me the coupon at the back of this book, and we can sit right down and figure out which strategies are going to work best for you to take care of you and your family today, tomorrow, and every day after.

Maybe you're still nervous about taking that final step. After all, big changes are hard, especially when your just getting started on them. To ease your mind, let me lay out exactly what a visit to my office will look like.

When you come into the office, the first thing you'll notice will be all the objects we have that celebrate Helen's life. I hope you'll get the chance to get to know her a little better then, although you already know so much about her from this book.

When we sit down together, we'll start by taking a look at one of your tax returns, as well as any of your current investment statements that you have. If you have some life insurance or long-term care insurance, bring all of that background information with you, but leave your checkbook at home. I'm not going to charge you anything.

In fact, I'm not going to ask you to make a decision on the spot or do anything. That first meeting is my time to hear you. You've read everything I had to say on the topic, now I need to hear from you. I want to know what your concerns are and how I can best assist you in moving forward.

Because, remember, I don't charge fees and I don't have products that charge fees. I'm not looking to sneak in a fee here or a fee there to get a little bit more out of you. As a fiduciary, it's my responsibility to make sure that you understand everything that I do. Personally, it's important to me that you know I'm not hiding anything from you. Anything you don't understand or you aren't comfortable with, you tell me, and your word always wins out.

Any conflicts of interest that I have, I can explain to you, and I will continue to explain until you can understand it. What all of that means is this: I don't work for anybody but you. You are hiring me to solve your problems, and I am going to use what I know are the best strategies available to do just that. Those strategies are simple. I can write them out in one sentence. What you need are safe, guaranteed, fixed, index annuities and life insurance that provides all the benefits that you've come to understand in this book.

I started off this book asking you if you wanted to be both brave and wise with your mortality. After you've embraced the fact that you are not going to get out of this life alive, you can begin to make wise decisions about how to protect yourself and your family going forward.

Since you're so wise now, at the end of this book, I doubt I need to go over this again, but here we go one last time. One of the wisest decisions you can make in your life is to learn from the wise farmer and his interaction with the IRS agent. It was that farmer who discovered the **5% Solution.**

That **5% Solution** is what I live by. I'll never take a cent from you that you were ever going to use. All we'll do is just take a little bit out of your Never Bucket, we'll pay taxes on that, and we'll be able to create a very large tax-free estate for that Harvest Bucket that your family will get, inheritance tax free, income tax free, estate tax free, at the end of your life.

The **5% Solution** is a powerful tool, and it allows me to help my clients achieve the three main goals they have when they enter my office: make their money safe, eliminate their fees, and when possible, keep them from going broke in a nursing home.

If you're still unsure of that, don't worry. I'm not going to force it on you. Come into the office, and we'll just talk. That first meeting (which, again, is free for you) is just about having a conversation. I'll take a few notes, I'll ask a few questions. I just want to find out what you are interested in doing, how I can help you, and whether the help I want to provide is something that you want to take advantage of.

If, at the end of our meeting, you decide, like most people, that you think I can do something to help you and your family, then I'll be very happy to bring you into what really is our family. At my business, we treat you very well. It's a small, family-owned business. I know all my clients by name, and I really appreciate my clients. To me, you're not a nameless, faceless entity as you are with a large corporation.

To me, your an individual with a family, with real and reasonable concerns about what your finances will look like for the rest of your life and what you can save for your family after you pass. This is important to me, because I know that everyone is someone's Helen.

So, just come into my office, any time, and bring all your financial info. Let's find a way to take care of you and your family today and tomorrow, no matter what happens.

Appendix

Advantages of Annuities

Tax Deferred Growth: The interest earned is not taxed until it is touched. Your funds grow tax deferred.

Safety: Annuities are among the most guaranteed and safe investments available.

Avoid Probate: Annuities transfer to a beneficiary without the need for probate.

Income: At any time, annuities can change from a savings or accumulation vehicle to an income vehicle. Annuities can provide an income that cannot be outlived.

Estate Planning: Annuities are used in estate planning to help protect assets in the event of a long-term care situation.

Interest Income: Interest is available for income any time after the first 30 days of the deposit. The interest can be withdrawn monthly, annually or quarterly.

Death Benefit: Your beneficiaries always have numerous options for income and other settlements in the event of death.

Fees: No contract fee or sales commissions are deducted from your premiums.

Comparison: Interest rate on annuities is usually higher than bank CD's or other fully guaranteed products.

Access: Unlike bank CD's, you have access to your funds during the interest earning time period.

Disadvantages Annuities

Penalty for Early Withdrawal: During the guaranteed period, if you withdraw more than the contract allows, a penalty is imposed. This penalty can be voided by using the contract as an income (pension type income) or as a death benefit paid to a beneficiary. Most annuities allow you to withdraw 10% of the account value annually without penalty.

Tax Penalty Prior to Age 59 1/2: Access to funds prior to age 59 1/2 in any tax deferred investment, including an annuity, may be subject to a tax penalty of 10%.

About the Authors

Philip Richardson and his wife Cathy live in Elizabethtown with their three children, Jordyn, Halle and Philip Jr. Philip and Cathy enjoy taking early morning walks and enjoy watching the sun rise across the fields. Philip says, "Living out in the country is like being on vacation every day. We are early risers and enjoy each other's company before heading into the office."

George and his wife Jennifer live in Lancaster with their two Yorkies. George and Jennifer enjoy spending time at the shore and often travel to Myrtle Beach to visit with family. They especially enjoy walking on the beach and dipping their toes in the ocean.

Philip and George have educated thousands of seniors on protecting their money from market losses, avoiding money management fees, keeping their spouse out of poverty, not going broke in a nursing home, avoiding tax mistakes seniors make and avoiding the delay and expense of probate. They are sought after speakers who bring a unique view to the financial world you won't get from most advisors. They have also been on the radio with a weekly show discussing how to implement the strategies they recommend to seniors.

Let Philip and George help you ensure your finances during your golden years are stress fee. Regardless of what the future may bring, by working with Philip and George you'll be Winning at Retirement.

Made in the USA
Middletown, DE
07 April 2019